THE BLUE STEPPES

Copyright © 2018 Read Books Ltd.
This book is copyright and may not be
reproduced or copied in any way without
the express permission of the publisher in writing

British Library Cataloguing-in-Publication Data
A catalogue record for this book is available from
the British Library

THE BLUE STEPPES

ADVENTURES AMONG RUSSIANS

BY
GERARD SHELLEY

PREFACE

IN WRITING THESE PAGES, I have endeavoured to throw a light on those dark forces which were so long fermenting in Russia and produced the most staggering of upheavals. Bolshevism is not the product of air or angels. It was of long growth in the soil of Russia and was showing its features in the lives of the intelligentsia long before it acquired political power. So I refrain from giving soulless lists of statistics, undertakings, railways, tables of imports and exports and the rest of the material scaffolding. It is not the house, not the style of its decorations, nor the dresses of its people, but their actual lives, thoughts, outlook and reactions which are really instructive and decisive. For it is by these forces alone that heaven or hell is made, society is run or ruined and the unembodied theories of doctrinaires are put to the acid test. Governments and theoreticians may come and go, but the people go on for ever. And it is because Russians are such confirmed lovers of theory that their actual lives are so interesting. For the rest, I will quote Merejkovsky's words to Western Europe:

"We resemble you as the left hand resembles the right; the right hand does not lie parallel with the left, it is necessary to turn it round.

The Blue Steppes

What you have, we also have, but in the reverse order ; we are your underside. Your genius is of the definite, ours of the infinite. You know how to check yourselves in time, to find a way round walls, or to return ; we rush onward and break our heads. It is difficult to hold us back. We do not go, we run ; we do not run, we fly ; we do not fly, we fall. You love the middle ; we, the extremities. You are sober ; we, drunken. You, reasonable ; we, lawless. You guard and keep your souls, we always seek to lose ours. You are in the last limit of your freedom ; we, in the depth of our bondage, have almost never ceased to be rebellious, secret, anarchic. Not in reason and sense, in which we often reach complete negation—nihilism—but in our occult will, we are mystics."

Following are my experiences.

CONTENTS

		PAGE
	PREFACE	7

CHAPTER

I.	IN THE TRAIN	11
II.	A FAMILY OF NOBLES	29
III.	A FAMILY OF NOBLES (*continued*)	42
IV.	THE END OF A FAMILY OF NOBLES	54
V.	THE ERA OF RASPUTIN	66
VI.	DAYS AND NIGHTS WITH RASPUTIN	81
VII.	THE HOUSE IN THE HORSEGUARDS' ALLEY	98
VIII.	THE HOUSE IN THE HORSEGUARDS' ALLEY (*continued*)	115
IX.	THE HOUSE IN THE HORSEGUARDS' ALLEY (*continued*)	133
X.	THE HOUSE IN THE HORSEGUARDS' ALLEY (*continued*)	146
XI.	A GARDEN OF EDEN	166
XII.	THE HOMES OF THE MIGHTY (PETROGRAD)	184
XIII.	THE HOMES OF THE MIGHTY (MOSCOW)	198
XIV.	A MIXED HOUSE	230
XV.	A BAG OF DIAMONDS	249
XVI.	OUT OF THE JAWS OF HELL	262

THE BLUE STEPPES

Chapter I

IN THE TRAIN

PEOPLE WHO CAME from Russia would never cease talking about the mysterious beauty of the country they had left. Not all the splendour of the haunts of fashion in Western Europe could still their longing for the land that lay, deserted and snow-bound, so far away. They brought with them their Bacchanalian zest in enjoyment, their caviare and their regrets, and Western Europe offered them its choicest pleasures for their ringing roubles. But their thoughts were ever turning to the blue steppes, the kingdoms of flatness and poverty, moujhiks and vodka, grand dukes and anarchists.

They were enchanted by the blue steppes. "Space!" they would exclaim, flinging their arms wide apart. "Here in Western Europe everything is so narrow, so conventional. One is afraid to be free."

I felt at the time that there must be a great idea behind such yearnings and such affection for unbounded freedom of conduct. I caught the Russian fever. I wanted to go to Russia. In 1913, when the chance came, I set out with all the curiosity and courage of Eve approaching undaunted the fruity tree. I thought I might enjoy the broad, spacious and unfettered sense of living which my young Russian friends raved about during their voluntary exile in conventional Europe.

Knowing but a few words of Russian at that time, I had found my journey from Warsaw to Koursk a long and tedious imprisonment in a slow, musty-smelling train, from the windows of which I could see nothing but dreary plains and miserable hovels. The little grey, lopsided huts of the villages with their haunting look of ugly squat spiders, joyless and as hopeless as blind, tattered beggars by the wayside, failed to compensate me for my ignorance of the language, in which my fellow passengers were pouring out endless cascades of hissing, gurgling, colliding sounds. Only when the golden domes of Kiev loomed into view, sparkling and flashing in the brilliant sunshine against the deep blue sky, did I feel a sense of relief from the growing burden of monotonous misery. The long grey pall that covered the plains of Russia burst at last into a gorgeous pattern of gold, blue, white, red and silver. As the train passed over the broad, sparkling Dnieper, I heard the bells of the monastery churches scattering their deep-toned notes on the quivering, warm air. There were lots of little boats on the river with staggering men dressed in blue and pink tunics playing harmonicas and singing in harmony. The phantom pallor of nude bodies splashed the distant green banks. A few minutes later the vast plain laid out its dreary pall again.

Kiev brought me relief in more than one sense. Just as I had decided to expect no break in the view until the train reached Kharkov, and was preparing to take a nap, a young man staggered along the corridor, bumping against the walls with two cumbersome cloakbags. His puckered brows and flustered look suggested all the annoyance he must have felt in passing from wagon to wagon, with an occasional lurch from the jolting train to batter his shins and a sudden heave to assist him in prodding the encumbering humanity in the corridor with his two gigantic bags. The train was crowded. The ceaseless rookery of prattling tongues, all wagging as fast as they could and running all the gamut of human tones, would have convinced even the solitary horse that tossed its head and dashed snorting away over the plain at the sight of the train, that it was loaded with a strange tribe of animals. Silent and forsaken among them, I felt as though I would have changed places with the horse.

" If there is nothing out of the ordinary in all this," I thought, " nothing but the common everyday chatter, then I think it's a miscarriage of Providence for people to have to knock one another's ears about and rend the atmosphere with these terrific sounds. What a waste of time and energy! Surely the people that treat one another with such emotion must be nervous wrecks at forty."

Perhaps this thought was due to my despondent mood. I had been trying to spell out the letters of the terrible declaration over the door :

"Vospreshtchayetsia kurit."

I had looked them both up in my pocket dictionary. In plain English it meant "smoking forbidden." But I fancied the words were merely put up for poetic adornment, for everyone about me was smoking like unweened devils. The greasy floor was littered with burnt matches and the little charred corpses of the paper holders peculiar to Russian cigarettes. I could plainly see that most things in Russia ended in smoke, prohibitions included. Perhaps all the terrific chatter pouring out from scores of energetic jaws had just as much significance as the shoals of littered fag-ends on the floor and had its origin in the same spiritual necessity.

I wondered all the more because my Russian friends in exile had assured me that the Russian had more "soul" than other mortals and far more "feeling" than I considered sensible. It had always been instilled into me that uncontrolled feeling was a bit of a nuisance in the conduct of life, but my friends had always referred to it as their greatest possession and delight. Yet I knew sufficient of Russian life to realize that it could also boast of its unfeeling governors and generals, its hardened police agents, its ruthless Bazarovs among the socialist intelligentsia, and its merciless rebels among the peasants. Were all these just the counterpart of the cult of unbounded feeling, the unavoidable outcome of spiritual anarchy, the cruel, monstrous balance necessary to preserve the equilibrium of society?

I thought of all this as I listened to the tones and watched the manners of my fellow passengers. There was nothing else for me to do. I had no book to read save my pocket dictionary, my bag of books having disappeared in Warsaw owing to the mistake of a Frenchwoman, who had taken it away and finally left it in the care of the stationmaster. It had to remain there till I got to my destination.

On the seat opposite sat a queer-looking middle-aged man with a woman I took to be his wife and a boy in uniform, who was evidently their son. From the constant supplications addressed to him by his mother, I gathered that his name was Serge.

"Seriojha! Seriojha!" she stormed, whined, raved, threatened, wailed, implored, besought and cajoled in succession. I couldn't make out what it was all about, but it was an amusing revelation to me of the way in which domestic affairs were conducted in the ranks of the intelligentsia. In the space of ten minutes, Seriojha had pouted, snarled, distorted his features with all sorts of horrid expressions, disgorged a torrent of heated, crashing language, spat on the floor, and as far as I could make out, sent all the gods that be to Jericho. Father and mother alternated their Olympic thunders with abject supplication.

I can still see in my mind's eye their heaving bosoms, tortured faces and trembling outstretched hands, while in my ears rings the sound of their torn, tear-laden voices.

"Rahdi Boga! Rahdi Boga!" they kept repeating.

I looked in my pocket dictionary and saw that it meant "for God's sake".

To every "Rahdi Boga", Seriojha returned a terrible sound, half a hiss and half the struggling curse of a man who is being strangled:

"Kkkchchorrtoo!"

I looked it up in my pocket dictionary and saw that it meant "to the devil!"

"Sweet child!" I thought, watching the Mephistophelian furrows into which his face was contorted. Satanic violence seemed to fill the atmosphere. Sulphuric spirits seemed to ride the welkin.

At last the raging storm of emotions, hot, electric and torturing, dropped with a sudden death as though its valkyrian fury had spent itself in over-violence.

"Tookh!" said the man, casting the word out as though it had been a poison in his mouth and waving his hand sharply downwards as a sign of despair, resignation and contempt. "Naplevat! Naplevat!"

He staggered out into the corridor, mopping his brow and drawing a deep breath of pure, fresh air.

"Naplevat!" he kept muttering and waving his hand downwards as at something hideous, vile and contemptible.

I looked in my pocket dictionary and saw that the words meant "to spit on a thing".

Meanwhile tears began to flow copiously from the eyes of Seriojha's mother and her sobs gripped even my phlegmatic bowels. I wondered what heinous deed or intention of the boy it was that could call forth such a terrific whirlwind of futility, such a volcanic rending of the atmosphere and one another's nerves. I looked at Seriojha and saw that the furrowing fury had left his handsome features. A gentle look came into his eyes. He suddenly seized his mother in his arms and hugged and kissed her passionately.

"Prosti, mamochka! Prosti!" he kept repeating, his voice quivering with the tears of repentance and humility.

I looked in my pocket dictionary and saw that the words meant: "Forgive, little mother, forgive!"

Then Seriojha's father, having recovered from his mutterings of "naplevat", looked through the door and hurried in to share the kisses and embraces of forgiveness.

Seriojha stretched himself out on the seat vacated by his parents and allowed himself to be covered with a rug. A downy pillow was placed under his head and his mother's kisses and murmurs fell upon him in showers.

"Slava Bogoo!" his father kept repeating with great feeling, a look of relief and satisfaction beaming over his sallow, shapeless features.

I looked in my pocket dictionary and found that it meant "Glory to God!"

So the object of all the terrific tornado of emotions was to induce the boy to take a nap. Never before had I seen so much violence of feeling stirred up for so trifling a matter. Through it all I descried the dark, grim tyrant of anarchy, whipping up and torturing his unhappy victims with all their merciless egotism and futile lack of vision and control.

I should not have mentioned this incident if my ensuing experiences of Russian life had not taught me that the very same elements of attitude and feeling lay at the bottom of similar incidents which made up all the gruesome, overcharged, terrific picture of the every day life of the Russian intelligentsia.

The only bright spot in it was the reconciliation and outpouring of affection. But even that, I was soon to discover, was just an interlude until the demons of anarchy rent the atmosphere again. And seventy times seven were the forgivings and embracings and the same number of times the red furies raged. . . .

There could be only one form of government for people of such a temperament. To live by mood alone is to own a pitiless master.

In the Train

Hearing sounds of alarm further along the corridor, I went out to discover what was afoot. High words were pouring out of a coupé, before which a group of onlookers stood laughing and enjoying the scene. One little fat man among them amused me immensely. He wore a short green coat with brass buttons and a white peaked naval cap. When he took it off to scratch his head after a paroxysm of mirth, he disclosed a billowy pate flecked with the pepper and salt of closely cropped hair. At every fresh outburst of clamour or some sally of wit or invective, unintelligible to me, he would give his thick stumpy thigh a sounding slap and crumple with emotion, exclaiming " Chch . . . orrt ! " which I had just taken to mean " The Deuce ! "

I thought perhaps a band of actors were providing the passengers with gratuitous entertainment, although it sounded very much like an imminent general smash-up. I ventured to draw a little nearer, when suddenly there was the sound of breaking glass, followed by a score of high-pitched, excited voices all shrieking at once. The funny little man slapped his thigh with a force that seemed to indicate final and consummate satisfaction, rapped out " Chch . . . orrt " with all the emphasis of a Billingsgate porter, and staggered along the corridor like a man half-seas over.

I turned to get out of his way and collided with the young man I had previously seen pass down the corridor with his load of bags. I

The Blue Steppes

hastily apologized for my clumsiness. In a flash he had guessed that I was a foreigner. There was a look of haughty contempt on his clear-cut features. He soon enlightened me, however, that his dissatisfaction referred to other specimens of humanity than myself. He turned out to be a young German who was returning to his post in a bank at Kharkov. But he had no need to tell me his nationality, for he no sooner took off his hat than he revealed it at once. His hair was cropped to resemble the bristles of a hedgehog and I realized in a flash that I had found someone to talk to, even though the language was German.

He was equally glad to find a listener, to whom he could pour out some of the haughty, critical feelings which were surging through his breast.

Finding that he had been unable to secure a seat, I invited him to take a rest on mine in the stuffy coupé, where Seriojha lay endeavouring to sleep under the ceaseless murmurs of his meddling mother and father.

The cold, superior mask of contempt had settled on Herr Wegall's features, as he confided to me that he considered the Russian people had no honesty or honour.

"You'll find out for yourself pretty quick," he said. "Word of honour means nothing whatever in Russian and no one ever takes it seriously. In Russia, if one wishes to take an oath of honour that is valid, one must give the German word 'Ehrenwort'. Duty, order, virtue, logic—everything dissolves in Russia."

In the Train

"Then how does this vast country keep together?" I asked.

"The bulk will always be there and always hold together in some form," he replied. "But what order and greatness there is, relies on the German element. They are the salt of Russia. There are two millions of them altogether and they supply most of the governors and generals, directors and organizers. Take away the Germans and the Empire will collapse like a castle of cards."

The Teutonic tone of authority rang in his voice. I could see that he was fully convinced of the truth of all he had said and was supremely conscious of his part as a minor Kulturträger in the marches of Barbary. When I asked him whether there was any chance of the British taking their share in the task, he made a wry mouth and raised his brows satirically. From his pocket he drew out a small edition of Schopenhauer's works, and hastily turning over the pages with his long, thin fingers explained that he would quote that great philosopher's opinion of the value of British education. In a highly contemptuous voice, an indulgent smile of pity and derision hovering over his face, he read out a long tirade against the Anglican clergy and the stifling part they played in the education of Englishmen.

I listened patiently and then informed him that I had never passed through the hands of Anglican clergymen.

"That is interesting!" he replied, brightening up and seeming to imply that I had had a lucky escape. "Then that is why you speak German?"

"I have lived abroad from a very tender age," I assured him.

He asked me where I was going to and what had brought me to Russia.

"I have come to see the sights," I replied. "I have heard that Russia is like no other country on the face of the earth. Mysticism . . ."

He interrupted me with a very Teutonic "phut!" His pouchy lips curled up into an acanthus of contempt and sceptic derision.

"You'll find a lot of that," he said. "It's another name for chaos and lack of reason. *Keine Methōde* [he said these words with a delicious drawl on the *o*] and dirt and stinks are as incense to their god."

"Maybe they have no method," I replied, remembering that he and his compatriots reserved to themselves the honour of conferring it on the poor Russians. "*Aber die Seele!*"

I lingered on the last word with as sentimental an intonation as I could invent for the gratification of this child of Goethe.

"Soul!" he exclaimed.

I thought, however, that the subject could not be dismissed in such a characteristically Teutonic manner, and registered a vow that I would give it all my attention when I came into contact with Russians through the medium of their own language. And later events proved that I was right, for there is nothing in the world so surprisingly different as a Russian who makes himself known to you through the polite medium of French or English and the same man revealing himself in his native language. It is like a specious demi-mondaine who slips back into her native element when the eyes of the world are withdrawn from her.

When I mentioned to my companion that I was going to stay with Count Torloff, his eyes assumed a look of intense interest. Of course, he knew all about the Count. He was the foremost man in the Government of Kharkov and owned thousands of acres in the neighbouring Government of Koursk. Yes, I was certainly in luck's way, he assured me. He wished that he, too, might have the chance of spending a delightful time with the richest and most distinguished people in the province instead of going back to his stool in a provincial bank. But he did not appear to have found life altogether dull; at least, he had found time to hear all about the life of those whose lot he envied. He began at once to describe to me the private life of the Governor of Kharkov and his wife, of the Marshal of the Nobility, the Commander of the Garrison, the Chief of the Police and all the outstanding persons in authority.

They were strange, hair-raising tales, which I thought I had read somewhere on a sultry summer afternoon. As I listened to his eloquent descriptions—he was evidently glad to prepare me for any disillusionment regarding my preconceived views of Russia—I heard the laughter of women, the shouts of men, the clink of champagne glasses, the cries of alternative adoration and execration, the clash of swords, the cracking of horse-whips, the passionate voices of singing gypsies and over all, like a distant, plaintive echo, the cries of protest of ill-used men and women, the stifled wail of execrating lips and the sharp, sudden crack of rifles. . . .

I listened enchanted to all that my haughty German companion poured with malicious savour into my ears. How much of it was true, I hardly dared surmise, for I was more than ever anxious to start on my career of personal acquaintance with the strange, inimitable people whose doings gave so much variety to this monotonous affair called life. Stronger than ever was my resolution to learn the language and to make myself independent of interpreters and the treacherous service of a polite European language. I had been warned that the Russian nobles used French as a veneer with which to cover their native Tartardom. Having spoken French, German and Italian from a tender age, I felt sure I would have no difficulty in acquiring Russian. And experience was to teach me that the foreigner who investigates the strange ways of Russia, under whatever system of government, without a thorough knowledge of the language is like a fool in Petticoat Lane or an ass at the animals' concert. But once the language is mastered a world of terrible possibilities opens out before one. The limitations, the helplessness, the preconceived notions, fall away like the curtains of a hidden scene, and before one's bewildered eyes appears a rich reality, dark, fearsome and terrible in its crude, nauseating darkness, its fierce, blinding light and shameless barbarism, its shuddersome black shadows of grim violence and death, together with the glowing colours of pity and heroism, its fragrant blossoms of tenderness, love and endurance.

There was an interruption when the train stopped at a small station, and a terrific altercation began afresh in the Seriojha family. Not wishing to witness another scene, I clambered down on to the sandy platform.

Barefoot peasant girls, dressed in red and pink print frocks, with coloured kerchiefs tied over their heads, offered wild strawberries and eggs for sale. Old women held up little earthenware pans of pickled herring, sausages, and pickled gherkins and mushrooms.

My German companion bought some of the herrings and pickled stuff. Back in the train he insisted on my tasting the mushrooms. They were of the bolus kind, very thick and pulpy. I had already tasted something similar in a Russian restaurant in Vienna. I mentioned the fact to him.

" Quite likely," he replied. " There is quite a business in the Koursk Government pickling and exporting gherkins and mushrooms. These grow abundantly in the forests. The peasants gather them in the early morning and sell them to the landowners, who boil and salt them, put them into bottles and send them abroad. The Emperor of Austria (Franz Joseph) is particularly fond of them. You always see them on Russian tables as *hors d'oeuvres*. There's a funny old woman in the neighbourhood of Count Torloff, where you are going to stay. She makes a good income out of the mushrooms, though most of her trade is done with Petersburg and Moscow. No doubt you'll be taken to see her. She banks with my firm and has the reputation of being the meanest old woman in existence. She haggles with the peasants over the price of the mushrooms, and periodically lays all her servants under arrest on the charge of pilfering in the pantry. And poor devils, I shouldn't be surprised if they did. She herself weighs out their daily portion of black bread and, sprinkling it with a pinch of salt symbolical of traditional hospitality, quotes the Lord's Prayer to them with stern exhortations to be truly thankful. If an ounce is missing she has the servants locked up by the local guard and undertakes a systematic search of their boxes and belongings, and whatever money she discovers she confiscates. She declares it must have been come by illicitly, as she herself disposes of her servants' wages, investing one-third in our bank on their behalf and receiving the interest for herself as payment for her services to illiterate persons; one-third she lays out on clothes, buying the material and having it made up by her own maid into liveries on which she traces her coat of arms and sews on brass buttons with her crest. From the remaining third she deducts a sum to pay the maid for making the material up and to cover the cost of the buttons. The remainder is kept by her in reserve to pay for fines which she inflicts on them for all sorts of trespasses. She has a list of them, as weird as any brain could invent, hanging up in their rooms and quarters. She fines a servant ten copecks for failing to answer her handbell at once, which often happens, since she delights in sending the domestics to all the quarters of the globe on all sorts of wild goose errands. When the sum is exhausted she draws on that deposited at the bank. She rules them all with a rod of iron and swears at them like a trooper. They tremble and adore her. She has a grey moustache and two yellow teeth that dance perpetually up and down on her thick, protruding lower lip. She is devoted to a tall, massive ex-Guardsman of the Preobrajhensky Regiment. He is six-foot-five in height and as broad as a giant. Nikanor is his name, and whenever she gets into a temper, which happens about ten times a day, the house, the yard and the woods around echo her bellowing voice calling out ' Nikanor ! Nikanor ! . . .' And when he doesn't appear on the spot as quick as a jack-in-the-box, the air is rent by a terrible hiss : ' Sookin sin ! Sookin sin ! ' (son of a dog !). When at last he turns up, perspiring with haste and anxiety and mopping his brow with the great red handkerchief bearing

The Blue Steppes

his mistress's coat of arms in gold thread, he sinks down on his knees as she shrieks out curse and villainy upon him and cudgels him soundly with her knotty stick. The great fair, pale-eyed giant bleats for mercy : ' Forgiveness, Your Splendour ! ' and beats his head on the ground before her feet. Then at the end of the storm he humbly kisses her finger-tips."

Chapter II

A FAMILY OF NOBLES

I

WHEN I ALIGHTED from the train that had brought me from Kharkov, I found myself in the midst of a roaring crowd of sheepskin-coated moujhiks. The rank smell of their top-boots and rough clothing mingled with the fragrance of the vast fields of standing oats on one side of the rails and with the warm odour of the immense forest of pine-trees that stopped short, like an enormous towering wave, at the very edge of the narrow line.

I was at last on the soil of the Russian country, far away from towns and "culture". The puffing, wood-fed train rumbled away through the endless stretch of golden corn, tossing its white mane of smoke against the lark-loud, quivering blue sky, and drawing out from its fiery bowels a long, heart-moving, mournful sigh that rolled with hollow echoes through the deep, slumbering forest. What vastness! The breeze swept across the boundless steppe, hot with the odours of its long journey and the ardours of the sun. No hedges, ditches, or fences as in the country at home, no rows of

The Blue Steppes

stately elms or oaks to mark the boundaries. Here, everything was too vast, too far-flung for such adornment. Where trees grew, they grew in forests, boundless as the fields they bordered. No houses were in sight beyond the low buildings of the station, though at one far end of the horizon a long ribbon of smoke trailed slowly across the sky, as from an unseen liner on the boundless ocean. A factory, no doubt.

All around me swarmed moujhiks, shouting their greetings to one another and seating themselves on their snorting horses. They lashed them mercilessly, and, clattering over the cobbled yard, dashed off on to the soft, stoneless, sandy track. A bearded, long-haired priest, in a violet cassock with a large gold cross on his breast, entered a *brichka*, crossing himself piously as he drove off.

Standing alone on the deserted platform, I waited for a messenger from my friends to come for me. I looked round the yard, but could find no one. A brightly polished carriage of superior aspect stood there, deserted. A young man, dressed in conventional town attire, came up to me, introducing himself in English as Vassili Bodkin, of a neighbouring estate. He was, I discovered later, the son of the Tsar's physician. Offering me very kindly his help, he went into the little vodka-cabin at the back of the station and rounded up Simon, the coachman, and Emilian, the man-servant, who had been sent by Count Torloff to meet me. They were dressed in white liveries with crested brass buttons.

A Family of Nobles

Neither had ever seen an Englishman before, so they both opened wide their large, glassy eyes, shaking their heads and muttering something I could not understand. I asked M. Bodkin what they were saying. "They want to know whether you belong to a Turkish tribe and how many wives you have brought with you," he replied. "The peasants here are still under the impressions produced by the wars of Catherine the Great against the Turks. The peasant mind moves at the pace of centuries."

Hearing us talk English, the two men again shook their heads and made some mournful remark.

"They say Russian is the best language," M. Bodkin explained, "because it is understandable. Not like your bird's language no Orthodox soul can understand."

Thanking my rescuer for his kindness, I bade him *au revoir* and drove off in the carriage. For miles we glided over the sandy track, the horses' hoofs padding softly and sending showers of fine sand into our faces. Our way led through fields of fragrant corn, miles of beet, through shady, silent forests where the horses stopped to drink from a sedgy brook, then once more through hot, sunlit fields and across swampy heathland where flocks of geese splashed the green with white, where droves of wild horses galloped across the horizon with mad delight; past a band of red-skirted, kerchiefed peasant women, carrying glinting scythes across their shoulders and singing a high, wailing folk-song ; across a river-ford, where men and women bathed together in Eden innocence, until at last we entered a long row of white daub izbas, with gaily painted lattices, gathered all the dogs and urchins of the village in our trail, and dashed ahead with great speed and splendour to the open gates of the country mansion.

The whole family of Count and Countess Torloff, servants and retainers, trouped out to welcome me, a proceeding that was full of patriarchal cordiality, but a little embarrassing for a novice.

II

Situated in the midst of the steppe, on the top of a gentle grassy slope leading to a broad river, Count Torloff's house was an oasis of refinement. His prosperity was reflected in the houses of his workers, who crowded round his dwelling like the children of one big family. Indeed, they owed their happy conditions to his energy and foresight, for when he had inherited the estate, it was a poor, barren waste. He had borrowed money and started to cultivate beet, built a sugar refinery, and by this venture into capitalistic development was able to re-build his own house and erect up-to-date houses for his employees.

Count Torloff was Marshal of the Nobility and a member of the Council of Empire. Tall, stout and imposing, he was a typical Russian landowner of the old school. His dark, imperial beard and massive frame gave him rather a forbidding aspect, but there lurked in his clear, dark eyes a sprightly

COUNT TORLOFF WITH THE BANNER PRESENTED TO THE RUSSIAN TROOPS IN GALICIA.

[To face p. 32.

A Family of Nobles

glimmer that told of a large and affectionate heart. Indeed, he was a model parent, giving his sons nothing but the best of examples in all respects. Every morning he rose early, read a portion of the Scriptures and visited his sons to give them his morning greeting, and discuss the day's programme.

Countess Torloff was, likewise, a model parent. Nearing fifty years of age, she devoted herself to her sons' welfare as few women would care in other countries. Herself a woman of the highest cultivation (she detested " culture "), broad, generous and noble of mind, she maintained a staunch adherence to the principles and practices of the Orthodox Church, and encouraged her sons to walk in the same path, keeping up their interest as well as her own in science, art, politics, religion, philosophy and sociology.

It would be difficult for me to describe adequately the great hospitality I received at their hands. Everything that they could do for my comfort and entertainment was done, with a generous attention that was rather bewildering. There were horse-riding expeditions across the steppe and through the forests to neighbouring estates, usually ten miles distant, tennis, boating and picnics, the latter being arranged with the family of M. Bodkin, whom I had met at the station on the day of my arrival. The only trouble I experienced was due to the nightingales, which sang in scores on the bushes under my window with such a resounding richness and tirelessness that they prevented me from sleeping. I have never seen so many nightingales or heard such rapturous warbling as in that remote corner of the Government of Koursk.

In the warm, starry evening we would sit on the balcony, overlooking the cool, tree-bordered river, and play bridge, the tall ex-Guardsman menservants keeping the candles in trim. Stakes never went very high, on principle, as so many Russians being dare-all fatalists and caring nothing of risking their estates at the card-table, Count Torloff had imposed on himself and his family a definite rule, and showed that he had sufficient will-power to keep it.

About nine o'clock the hissing silver samovar would be brought out to the dining-table, at one end of the covered balcony, and there, in the mellow glow of the candles, wreathed about by the flitting moths, we drank fragrant tea and consumed delicious strawberries of the woods, which the barefoot village children had gathered and brought to the house for sale.

Till long past midnight one heard the splash of the bathing peasants in the river, by the creaking, wooden bridge, and sound of balalaikas and the piping voices of the village maidens singing folk-songs. Something wistful, melancholy and half-suffering seemed always to ring in those far-off voices, wafted up on the fragrant breeze from the far-flung steppes and mingled with the fiery raptures of the myriad nightingales.

A few days after my arrival, another English

visitor came. He was a venerable member of the Athenaeum, who was invited for a week and stayed a month. It happened in this way. Countess Torloff racked her brains to invent the choicest menus for the delectation of her venerable guest, who made up for the traditional "quiet hour" lifelessness of his club by displaying a discerning appetite for exquisite food. Bisque soup was on the menu one day and it was so well made that the venerable visitor ate more than was really good for him. He was obliged to remain in bed. When asked what he would like in order to get better, he replied : " I think a little bisque soup would restore my appetite and then I should feel quite well again ". It was thought inadvisable, however, to indulge this fancy, but after his recovery he so insisted on tasting once more that delicious soup that Countess Torloff restored it to the menu. As a result of this generosity, he was obliged to take to his bed for another week. On recovery he begged once more for the delightful liquid. His request was granted with much secret misgiving, and to the consternation of his host and hostess, the dear old man had to take to his bed for yet another week. Everyone was in despair, thinking he would remain for ever. Fortunately a timely letter arrived inviting him to another estate in the Baltic Provinces, and thither he went, being largely dependent on invitations for his means of existence.

About a fortnight after my arrival I was asked to go to a funeral at a neighbouring estate.

Questions elicited that it was the funeral of the very woman I had hoped so much to see. The description of her tallied exactly with the picturesque details given me by my chance companion on the train to Kharkov. I was very sorry to have missed the chance of seeing her alive, but decided to take the opportunity of witnessing a Russian funeral.

We drove over to the estate, which lay at a distance of some twenty versts. Everyone who knew Agripina Dimitrievna was certain she would be as original in death as she had been in life. Driving up the avenue of birch-trees, and catching sight of the white, wooden columns before the door of the wooden house, and between them the tall figure of Nikanor, the ex-Guardsman manservant, one almost seemed to hear the dead woman's masterly voice calling out from the top of the steps: "Nikanor! Ni-ka-norr!" and muttering wrathfully: "Son of a dog! son of a dog!"

We discovered on arrival that the body had already been taken into the village church close by, where a service was about to begin. A host of mourners, nobles, servants and peasants, waited about, chattering and gesticulating. In the long dining-room stood the table with the funeral bakes and decanters of marsala. When all were assembled the last will and testament of the deceased woman was read. It had been her wish that the contents of this document should be revealed before anyone set out for the church, where, in accordance with the Russian custom, her body was to lie in the uncovered coffin until the solemn moment when the loving mourners took leave of the beloved departed one for the last time. In her testament she dwelt on that moment with strange insistence, describing with savoury eloquence the loving, sorrowing looks of those who mourned for her dead body, their heartfelt protestations of grief, their fervent prayers for the repose of her soul. But before that happened she would sift the wheat from the chaff. She laid it down that her will was to be read beforehand, so that none should mourn over her dead body who had shown no care for it alive, that none should protest the grief of their hearts as a cloak for their expectations in her will, that none should offer prayers for the repose of her soul who had offered none for her welfare and peace in life.

As this was read out in a solemn, chanting voice by the thin-faced lawyer, a quivering silence electrified the assembled mourners. Eyes met eyes and turned quickly aside. Then somebody whispered into his neighbour's ear and the whole company cried out " Sh-sh-sh!" with indignation. The hot summer sunshine was pouring in through the open windows, casting a mocking glow over the taut features of the mourners, while the swarm of flies on the whitewashed ceiling danced and buzzed at every opening of the door by the peeping servants.

At last, having lashed about her with a vigorous

hand, the testatrix came to the distribution of her estate, advising all those who were dissatisfied to stay away from the last rites. She left a cottage and a pension to Nikanor, who had served her " like a faithful hound ", trebled all the savings she had extracted from the servants as a lesson in thrift, gave them a year's wages, and left the rest of her estate to the one man she was to have married, but never did. She directed she should be buried in the white satin gown that had been prepared for her wedding, and requested her would-be husband to place in her hands a bouquet of white lilies such as she would have carried had she been crowned his bride.

Such tenderness, such romantic memories in that poor, crusty heart! Such a glow of fervid hopes under that hard, wrinkled surface! Such wistful gentleness concealed behind those hard eyes, that had made a household tremble, behind that terrible voice that had scattered curses right and left, behind those claw-like hands that had laid so often about with the knotty walking-stick! How could anyone keep back the fountain of tears? Hot and fast they fell, stalwart men and proud women shedding them alike.

Whatever the disappointments, whatever the previous feeling of the mourners had been, none stayed away from the last rites. They passed into the church with streaming eyes, crossing themselves a hundred times and murmuring prayers without end. As I, the last, left the room in the old house, I looked back and saw the swarm of summer flies on the white ceiling dancing like a thousand imps in the draught from the open door, and as I walked away, their excited buzzing seemed to me like the faint laughter of the ghost of the woman, who in that room had put piety into the hearts of her survivors with an invisible rod of iron. . . .

In the gaudy church, the priests in their gorgeous copes were swinging censers and droning before the ikonastasis. In the centre of the nave stood the open coffin. The wax-like face of the ill-fated bride seemed to express a gentle smile. In her hands was a cross with a bunch of beautiful lilies, laid there by the one-time lover. After thirty years of absence, since he defaulted from the proposed marriage, he had returned for the funeral of his luckless bride. He was now governor of a provincial town. Only nine days before her death he had written to say he would like to renew her acquaintance, and was about to set out when the news of her sudden death arrived. Now he stood at the head of the mourners, desolate, and with head bowed down.

The priests droned, waved the censers, and waddled about in and out of the doors of the ikonastasis, like a religious hide-and-seek, crossed themselves and bowed, stroked their beards and shook their long locks. The choir sang sweetly, now bursting into loud calls for mercy, now sinking their voices to a whisper. All the while the tapers burnt ghost-like in the incense-laden haze, shot through by shafts of twirling sunlight from the high windows. Peasants pressed forward on all sides, filling the hot, stifling air with musty odours of leather and stale clothing.

The fat deacon, straggle-bearded and pale-eyed, growled from the depths of his bowels and waddled about. A surly, dazed look was on his freckled face. The stifling heat and odours seemed to make him stagger. Once when he incensed the ikon of the Virgin, the bottom of the thurible struck the image and sent out a shower of live charcoal.

The droning and waddling went on. It seemed to have no end, to lead nowhere. Suddenly a terrible thing tore a great shriek from the throats of the assembled mourners. Waddling round the bier, the half-dazed deacon caught his waving censer against a lighted taper. In a flash it toppled over, plunging its tiny flame into the lace and frills of the white wedding dress. In a moment the bier was a mass of flames. . . .

I can smell it even now. Twelve years have passed since the day I was fated to see it, but never can I drive from my memory the sight of the flames leaping from the flimsy wedding dress, the pungent odour of burning hair, the ghastly shrieks of the terrified mourners and, above all, the enormous round, white eyes of the unhappy man who was her " might have been ".

He stood in the midst of the howling panic as silent, stock-still and aghast as the pillar of salt which was Lot's wife, with his face turned, like hers, towards the object of his dearest thoughts, on which a dread, consuming fire had flashed like a bolt from the blue. The memory of that day is the first of many pinned by my experiences in Russia like a dark, odorous and mournful shadow on my soul. . . .

The deacon had, it was afterwards revealed, taken his share of the marsala in the dining-room while the mourners were in the study listening to the reading of the will.

Chapter III

A FAMILY OF NOBLES
(*Continued*)

I

COUNT TORLOFF lived at Bekino with his married brother and sister. These had their own houses and families at a distance of forty yards from the central house, so that one received the impression of a very close, patriarchal pitching of the family tents. Wishing to see everything and know everybody, I made the acquaintance of the village priest, his wife and family of fifteen, the village schoolmaster, a delightfully well-read, balanced man, who was the author of several works on botany, and lived in a neat little log cabin by the schoolhouse. The workers invited me to their houses and I often had tea with them, sitting round a well-scrubbed table on hard benches and talking by the hissing samovar. I practised my first steps in Russian on these good souls, and they repeated the names of things to me with a patience and goodwill that were all the more lovable because they were for no reward. It was not until the following year, after I had spent a considerable time at the university of Kharkov and could speak Russian fluently, that I began to penetrate the mystery of their nature. Then it was that I discovered the strange contrasts that flashed before one with startling suddenness, the passionate excitement and gaiety, the deep melancholy and despair, the gentlest manner and the most brutal violence. The same person would show the two faces within the space of five minutes, enchanting one with the most generous kindness and repelling one with the exhibition of wildest ferocity. The savagery among these gentle-ferocious people was terrible. Not a week passed but some poor corpse was fished out of the river, stabbed or bound hand and foot, some bread-earner was done to death along the tracks, in the forests, or across the thresholds of the vodka cabins. Watching them dance and sing before their pretty white izbas, or kissing the cross held out by the village priest in church, one could hardly believe their hearts would flash out such consuming lightnings, their hands perform such murderous deeds, or their lips express such atrocious blasphemies and obscenities. The latter were never punishable by law, and on all sides one had to listen to the desecration of every possible person or thing.

On the other hand there were cases where the poor helped the poor with heroic self-abnegation. I once went into an izba and found a family of twenty-three children! So many of them were of the same age that the poor mother must have had triplets time after time. I made inquiries and discovered that a brother of the peasant had been killed, leaving a motherless family of seven, another brother had got drunk and fallen into the river, leaving a family of ten, whose mother had forthwith disappeared. All these orphans were taken into the two-roomed izba and looked after by the poor man and his wife.

"We hoped the Lord would take the little ones," the woman said to me. "Here lots of babies die from flux. Every day the church bell rings for a little one. But no! the Lord wills these little chicks should live. What to do? Life is a sad business. To us, barin, it is predestined we should suffer. Christ was tortured. He busied himself, worked, suffered. God knows, we save our souls. Sometimes the food is not enough for all the hungry mouths, but we go without ourselves. The big ones are growing up. Already they go to work in the refinery, in the fields. Vanka is a clever boy. He is the quietest of the lot. He reads. He is to enter the office. He wants to learn, to become a student."

She showed me the room where they all slept, father and mother, the family and the orphans. Some slept on the stove, the rest on the floor. Yet the room was not more than ten feet square. This good woman made every scrap of clothing for this great family herself, growing, retting and dressing the flax, spinning and weaving, cutting and sewing. The eldest boy made shoes from birch-bark for them all. Except for occasional presents from Count Torloff, she had managed to do everything for the household on the small wages her husband earned at the flour mill, though now the earnings of the elder ones helped to satisfy the waxing appetites of the growing orphans.

In almost every izba I entered, I discovered orphans taken into the family and cared for on a level with the rest of the numerous children.

Now and again one came across sour-looking, surly young men who talked for hours and hours about socialism and revolution. They were chiefly the sons of peasants who had been to the universities, paying their way by all sorts of means, and living in attics, starving, never washing, and leading anarchic, gross lives, through which shone the dark jewel of their desire for the light of knowledge. "Knowledge is light" was their great watchword, caught from the lips of Tolstoy. Yet it was a strange conception of knowledge. They thirsted for the abstract, they pursued knowledge as something desirable in itself. And when they got it, they were like an ostrich that has hatched a crocodile. It led them to despise all existing society. With no idea of breeding, they spurned "bourgeois" manners, loathed the "bourgeois" professions. Their "knowledge" gave them nothing but dissatisfaction with the world. Despising all "bourgeois" means of gaining a living, they nursed themselves in endless dreams and talks of the future revolution and the socialist paradise.

Futile, garrulous and impractical, the only use they could find for their dearly acquired knowledge was to despise the only decent means of applying it and earning a livelihood. "The revolution! socialism! the abolition of the bourgeois!" Such was their constant cry, their futile dream. From such haters of practical society sprang the yearning for a proletarian world. Their peasant manners and origin clung to them always, and they seemed unable to part with them.

Perhaps for this the blame lay largely with the Russian aristocracy and the caste system, by which there were only two officially recognized and distinctly separate classes, the nobles and the peasants. The middle classes in the towns were still officially peasants domiciled in towns. And the arrogance with which the distinction was maintained by the bureaucracy, the haughtiness of the nobles, their constant and loudly expressed contempt for others, their boastings and vanities, their violent attachment to their privileges, must have lain at the bottom of this sullen mentality of the peasant-student.

In this respect, I remember the sudden revelation of a Russian trait which came to me a few days after my arrival at the estate of Count Torloff. We went out for a drive after tea. Countess Torloff invited me to sit in the carriage with her, while Count Torloff drove the second carriage, sitting on the box with the coachman. We took a long trip through the leafy forests, walked about on the odorous, thyme-covered, sandy steppe and then returned to the carriages. On the way back we encountered a man in a student's uniform sitting astride a droshky, a vehicle like a long pole on four wheels. He was driving on the right side of the track in accordance with the rule.

Wishing her carriage to pass straight on without making a detour, Countess Torloff called out to him : " Give the way ! "

The man took no notice of this order, but calmly continued his jolting road.

" Give the way ! Give the way ! " Countess Torloff called out again. Meeting with no response, she stopped the carriage and turned to her husband on the box of the carriage behind. She explained the matter to him indignantly. Throwing the reins into the hands of the coachman, he seized the whip and leaping down into the track, ran up to the man on the droshky, lashed him furiously with the whip, seized the reins of his horse and held the vehicle. The man lay in the dust, protesting his right to the road.

Ordering the coachman to mount the droshky and drive it to the house, Count Torloff returned to his box. That evening the student had to appear at the house for the return of his horse and vehicle, and was fined a large sum by Count Torloff, who was a justice of the peace, for " insulting behaviour to the nobility ! "

Such a procedure both surprised and grieved

me, for I held my hosts in great esteem and admired the general decency and charitableness of their lives. But I recognized, later on, that this sudden manifestation of autocratic power and fury was common to the nation in whatever class, and was one of the many mysterious facets of that strange collection of primitive and mystic forces, the Russian soul.

There was, of course, a common saying among Russians that " Russia needs the whip " and no doubt there were many who thought they had little else to do but apply it. But during the five years of my intimate acquaintance with the Torloff family, this was the only incident of its nature that I witnessed. Nevertheless, it was a revelation of prevailing views and relationships, and explains in some measure the intense hatred and demoniac feelings of so many of the Bolshevists when they assumed power. Such a state of mind is entirely foreign to Anglo-Saxon countries, and being a manifestation of the sinister spirit of hatred and merciless reprisals, is altogether out of keeping with the noble Anglo-Saxon mind, in its general aims and ideals. In that respect, the English-speaking countries have nothing to learn but all to lose in copying the methods of Russia.

II

Bekino was the village portrayed in Riepine's famous picture of the procession of the ikon, so I looked forward to seeing that event. The wonder-working ikon was to be brought from a neighbouring monastery on its way back to its final resting-place in the church at Koursk. Never once was it allowed to halt on that long journey, not once must it be allowed to rest or be carried otherwise than on running feet. From village to village it passed, the strong men going out to meet it half-way from the last village and carrying it on running feet half-way to the next. Already at five in the morning of the great day the bells of the village church were ringing, the big bells booming and the little lady bells tinkling up in the top of the tower like dancing jesters. Mounting our horses, we rode through the dusty village track, past the white izbas where the peasants were busy putting on their best kerchiefs and print frocks, past the waste ground, dotted with mounds and broken wooden crosses, where the village dead were buried and the village geese and pigs were foraging, across the long, creaking, rotten bridge and up the chalk hill to where one could see the long, long road winding away white and dusty into the golden horizon.

A warm breeze was blowing from the far-flung corn fields, where the larks were singing and soaring in the bright golden rays of the early sun. The fresh dew glittered like millions of fairy diamonds on the shaggy grass by the roadside. Up the sandy hill from the village came the stalwart peasants, young and old, yellow-haired and white, their pale eyes fixed on the quivering

The Blue Steppes

horizon where the white road dwindled into a dim speck. Barefoot women and children followed in hundreds, old, toothless, wrinkled hags hobbled behind, clutching their knotty sticks and smiling through their age-weary eyes. On, on, they went, down the dusty track towards the unseen ikon. . . .

We waited with the priests, deacons and blue-clad choir with incense and chants. Down the hill the bells of the church boomed and jingled, sending a rapturous joy through the clear, morning air. More people came from the village and stood with the waiting clergy, crossing themselves constantly and gazing towards the horizon. At last a faint something moved like a pin-head against the hem of the blue sky. A great shout rose from the throats of the watchers:

"They come! they come!"

With flushed faces and excited gestures, they rushed forward, turned back to the waiting priests, waved their arms, shrieked with joy, and rushed forward once more. No one seemed able to keep still. At last the surging wave of humanity from out the far horizon came nearer and nearer, growing blacker against the white road and streaming forward like a torrent. A great, flashing fire of gold burnt in the midst of them, where the rays of the rising sun struck the shrine of the holy ikon. It was like a fiery vessel rolling forward on a black torrent. On, on, they came. The nearer they approached the louder sounded the hum of the myriad voices and the wafted chanting of a monotonous invocation. Around the silent priests lay the sick, the halt and the blind of the neighbouring villages. Parents and friends stood by their sides, appealing in sad, monotonous voices for prayers on their behalf, chanting the history of each sufferer and describing his or her sufferings with pathetic eloquence.

At last the holy ikon, enclosed in a high, golden tabernacle and surrounded with lights and flowers, came rushing by, held aloft on two long horizontal poles. As the running carriers grew tired, they dropped out, yielding their places to fresh men. Mothers held up the children to see the wonder-working Virgin, glittering radiantly in her gem-studded robe of beaten gold. The sick and lame held up their hands in supplication, the priests chanted and the deacons swung their censers. Too soon the flashing ikon swayed by, carrying with it the fervid hopes and expectations of so many suffering hearts. The great roar of chanting voices, that had swelled up the long track like a mighty wave, passed with the multitude over the brow of the hill and subsided in the open plain below. But we did not follow the sight of the black, human stream. We turned to the sufferers who were struggling with their fallen hopes. Too many, alas, had been passed by, though a few showed marvellous signs of recovery. A "klikoosha," a sort of epileptic, ceased from her palsy and kissed the cross which the priest held out to her. A child with the whooping-cough (jumbled with half a dozen other children) was said to have recovered.

In the wake of the running crowd came pilgrims and beggars. Two white-bearded, blind men led each other, singing beautiful old folk-legends of the sufferings of Christ in delightfully mellow voices. When the last pilgrim straggled past, we turned our horses and rode into the slumbering forest, winding round the mossy tracks till we halted for goat's milk at the hut of the forest hermit. He was sitting at his door, reading laboriously an old Slavonic manuscript of St. John Chrysostom. When questioned about his reading, he answered with such deep-toned, rhythmic eloquence and wisdom that we were all surprised so much beauty could fall from the lips of this rugged old man of the woods.

Returning through the village, we found that the running pilgrimage of the holy ikon had left nothing but groups of chattering peasants before the doors of the white izbas. The bells of the church were booming and dancing their last joyful message, while the sick and the lame were returning to their homes.

I still remember vividly the peaceful beauty of that radiant morning, and hold like a fadeless treasure the picture of that glittering ikon on the shoulders of the running peasants, the enthusiasm, the prayers, the uplifted hands of the unfortunate, the joy of faith in the eyes of the old, wrinkled hags. Whatever the worldly estimate of these things may be, they strike a deeper note in the mysterious chords of the heart than the sight of a cup-tie crowd seething with enthusiasm at the passing of a ball. There, no hands are uplifted, no prayers are murmured and no old eyes are made joyful with the light of faith. . . .

Chapter IV

THE END OF A FAMILY OF NOBLES

I

WHEN WAR BROKE OUT, I was staying with the aged mother of Countess Torloff at her estate near Moscow. There, too, reigned that indescribable peace and remoteness which casts such a spell of melancholy over the Russian country. We had heard very little about the prospect of war. The Moscow newspapers arrived about five in the evening, but the affairs of the world seemed so far away that no one troubled about them. No great current of feeling could ever sweep through the Russian countryside as in smaller countries. For one thing, hardly five out of every hundred peasants could read. So the village teacher and priest had their cultured excitements all for themselves. One day at lunch a telegram arrived for Count Kuzoff, the officer brother of Countess Torloff. He read it, and springing up, declared to the astonished household that mobilization had been ordered. He left the table at once and went back to Petersburg.

On the day of the declaration of war, we

motored into Moscow and witnessed the great demonstrations. On the Kuznetsky Most, the mob invaded the shops of German piano dealers and threw Bechstein pianos from the upper storeys. Everywhere bands were heard playing " God Save the Tsar ", while people wept, embraced and knelt in the streets. Russia seemed to leap out of herself. Alas, that it was too fierce a fire !

We motored back to Kharkov by the eternal macadamized causeway that runs for hundreds of miles like a straight, white ribbon through the vastest stretch of black earth in the world. To find a single stone that had not been imported by man was almost as rare as finding a diamond.

At intervals we paid toll at the toll-gates. All the peasants' horses shied and bolted at the sight of the motor-car. For miles and miles one saw nothing but the harvest fields, the vast forests, and here and there, the straggling thatched huts of the villages like companies of grey mice. We stayed the night at Orel, consumed excellent beefsteaks with Worcester sauce and continued our journey under the clear smile of the rising sun. Once more there stretched before us the long, interminable way, the interminable fields, the dark forests. Here and there we passed pilgrims trudging along with crook and bundle, their eyes fixed glassily on the never-ending trail. Monotony, monotony, on every side as far as the eye could see, and that for hundreds of miles ! I do not wonder the Russians take to vodka, especially when the enormous plain lies like a silent desert of snow for eight months of the year. And the peasant student, returning to his native village with no other society but that of the " benighted " peasants, was inevitably held in the grip of this vast, grey plain and could find no other culture to suit his sullen heart.

In Kharkov, after the outbreak of war, I acted as interpreter for various groups of prisoners of war, who were being distributed over Russia. My knowledge of Italian was particularly useful for dealing with the Austro-Italian soldiers. I also censored letters in foreign languages and was surprised to find that the German bank clerk I had met on the train the year of my arrival was sending information about the strength of the Russian reserves and their proposed movements, details of the ammunition supplies and the output of the local factories. How I discovered this was almost a miracle. The letter was addressed to a bank in Stockholm and read just like an ordinary banking letter.

A chattering friend happened to drop in to see me as I was reading the letter through. It was written in German. I laid it down casually on the table and listened to my friend's animated description of the French victories. He unfolded a map and began tracing the movements of the German armies in their lightning sweep towards Paris. In his excitement he laid his lighted cigarette on the bank's letter. Whisking it off, I looked to see whether any damage had been done. There was a small brown spot in between the typewritten lines. To my surprise, I noticed that this spot revealed a couple of letters in German schrift. A further application of heat disclosed a secret communication between the lines of the whole letter, written in invisible ink. The letter being addressed to a Stockholm bank, it must have been expected by a man who knew what to find between the lines.

The German bank clerk was questioned about the matter, but no action against him was taken. The pro-German influence was too strong in official quarters, especially among the military. Had he been a Russian, he would probably have paid the penalty, but Germans in Russia were looked up to as models of honesty, and they enjoyed a privileged position even during the war, because the ruling officials of German blood and pride would not suffer any diminution of German prestige in the eyes of the Russian people.

Truth compels me to state that I noticed among the official classes a tendency to insult and ridicule the people who came within their power. This tendency reached diabolical proportions under Bolshevism, so I rather think it is ingrained in the Russian nature. Russians are such congenital anarchists, that once they hold power they become cruel tyrants. There was certainly no blood lust and infernal hatred among the old official classes as I later on observed and personally experienced among the Bolshevist tyrants, but the attitude and frame of mind from which these manifestations sprang were clearly discernible.

The Blue Steppes

At the beginning of the war many humbler Russo-Germans changed their names to Russian ones. To do so they had to petition the Tsar, which meant, of course, the bureaucracy. No difficulty was put in their way. Germans were always considered and treated as "superior persons". But when simple Russians applied, they met with callous snubs. There is a typical case in my personal knowledge. A young peasant's son had worked his way through the university and fulfilled his ambition to be a doctor. The name he was born with passed very well in the primitive life of the peasantry, where no social inconveniences were suffered. But entering on his career as a doctor, the young man found his name a drawback, particularly as he had specialized in obstetrics. His name was Nyezakonorojhdionny, which translated means Illegitimate. There are in England families who are very proud of their historical name of Bastard, but this young doctor did not like the prospect of advertising himself as " Dr. Illegitimate, specialist in midwifery ". He, therefore, petitioned for a change of name, with the customary formula of " your most humble, loyal subject, casting myself at your feet ", etc.

When the petition was granted, it was left to the bureaucracy to decide the future name. In this case, they imposed on the doctor, "in the name of the Autocratic Emperor of all the Russias " the name of Sinyepoopoff, which translated means " Blue-navel ".

There were shrieks of laughter whenever the

The End of a Family of Nobles

bureaucrats related this to one another. To me it seemed a revolting abuse of power, but to them it was amusing. The difference between them and their Bolshevist successors seemed to be that the latter carried this hideous trait to diabolical heights. The lust to make fun of, to torture the people in their power, seems to me the principal idea of Russian despotism. It was carried out by Ivan the Terrible, by Peter the Great, never died altogether even under milder autocracy, and burst out afresh with medieval frightfulness under the domination of the merciless Bolshevists. One hardly ever escapes it even in the best of Russians, for those who revolt against this tyrannical trait almost always take refuge in mysticism, acknowledging the terrible yoke and pleading that it is Russia's mystical destiny to suffer. It was curious to note how it often went hand-in-hand with the most delicate fancifulness, poetry, music and gentleness of manner. For any real comparison one must go to the romantic calm of a great sea, which conceals beneath its alluring surface the other aspect of raging waters and the fury of the tempest. The Russian revolution is hardly a revolt against Capitalism, but against the terrible psychological nightmares bred in the Russian mind by ages of tyranny.

II

Occasionally I was asked to accompany wagon-loads of material, such as gas-masks, woollen socks, shirts and other comforts for the soldiers in the trenches, fashioned by patriotic women and girls in the various teaching establishments and sewing circles. They were sent down to the Galician base under the auspices of the Red Cross Society. I did this work for a considerable period, but resigned at last owing to the wholesale abuses which begun to sweep the entire organization of supplies. Not only were there grave, appalling cases of peculation, but a revolting disregard for the lives of the unfortunate soldiers. Rascally contractors in high places did not hesitate to supply blank cartridges for the army. In the case of the woollen comforts and gas-masks for the army in Galicia, I was horrified to find that on arrival with my trust at Brody or Lemberg, it was sold to the Jewish speculators who abound in that country. These in their turn extracted the last copeck from the poorly paid soldiers for the woollen socks and scarves, shirts and gloves, etc., although all of them had been furnished gratis by the patriotic women and girls in the far-off home districts. The Russian officials were highly temptable and the unscrupulous Galician Jews were ever ready " to do business ". The unhappy Russian peasant soldier either had to yield up his last copeck or pass that terrible winter with inadequate clothing, even when he penetrated heroically across the snow-covered heights into Hungary. My protests being of no avail, I gave up the job of safeguarding Red Cross material to the base, since I was merely conveying it into the jaws of sharks. When I complained to the chief official he shrugged his shoulders, laid his hand on my shoulder and said, with a gentle smile of commiseration: "What to do, dear friend? Here, everybody does it. Do you not know what Turgueniev said about it? 'Every little bee likes to take a little sip from every little flower.' So we. It is not important. You see, it is not shedding of blood. Don't worry your little noddle, dear friend."

So I gave up that work and, knowing several languages, offered my services to the British War Office, who were in need of British interpreters. They sent me in reply a printed form declaring " they had received thousands of similar offers, but had noted my name ". It remained in notable obscurity for ever after. I turned once more to the Russians, who, in spite of all their defects, had no such nonsense as noting one's name, or sending out printed forms. I kept the form. It served me in good stead after the revolution, for when a zealous Bolshevist commissar suspected me of being a spy because I knew Russian so well, I proved to him, by means of the War Office's printed form, that it was precisely my knowledge of foreign languages which prevented me from being employed by the British, for very few of those sent out to Russia knew Russian.

When my Russian friends used to ask me why I preferred to work for the Russians, I simply pointed to the framed printed form on the wall. It was through Count Torloff's kindness that I was given a chance of using my languages for the work of

The Blue Steppes

interpreting and translating in connection with the prisoners of war. I was grateful for this task, for all my efforts to go as interpreter to the Italian front with the British expedition were in vain, although I had been brought up in the neighbourhood of the Lake of Garda and knew the war district well.

Nevertheless, by working for the Russians, I was fated to witness the end of my good friends, Count Torloff and his brother.

In April 1918, having been to visit old friends in Kharkov, I made a trip into the country to see Count Torloff and his family. The Bolshevists were in power and already staining the soil of Russia with torrents of innocent blood.

The factories were in the hands of soviets, while the large corn-producing and beet-growing estates were taken and divided up by the peasants. In the case of Count Torloff's beet-sugar refinery, it was obvious there must be a conflict between the peasants who claimed the land in order to satisfy their "land famine" and the workers at the refinery, who would have no sugar to refine if the beet-growing estate was broken up. The estate and the refinery were one entity. Whatever may have been the real motives of the factory workers, whether, as they declared, they wished the management to go on as before in Count Torloff and his brother's hands because of their own incompetence, or whether they wished to make a stronger case against the peasants, the fact remains that they made Count Torloff's brother president of their

The End of a Family of Nobles

Soviet and looked to him for guidance. But there were two other agitating individuals on the scene. They were M. Bronstein, the works manager, and M. Gurevich, a student who had been invited by Count Alexander Torloff to coach his sons for the Lyceum examination. Both these persons were Jews, and had been given their positions without any discrimination of creed or race.

After the revolution the two men declared themselves ardent Bolshevists and set out to assert their power over the whole estate and refinery. Perhaps it was to counter them that both the peasants and the workers sank their differences for a while and looked to their former masters for assistance.

Bronstein and Gurevich were furious at the action of the workers and peasants, and, declaring that they alone were true representatives of Soviet authority, started to secure their nefarious ends by drastic means. Gurevich went to Kharkov to the Red Army. A detachment of Red Guards were sent down, and, lest they should alarm the workers, were secreted at the little railway station at which I had alighted five years previously. Gurevich was with them and telephoned to the country house to say that a deputation was waiting at the station and wished to discuss affairs with the Counts Torloff. At the same time a number of soldiers arrived and ordered the people of the house to drive to the station. In the copse known as Malenki Bor, Count Torloff and his male relations were suddenly ordered out of the carriages and shot dead, their blood-stained bodies lying ghastly on the ground. ...

That day the terrified widows gathered their children about them and fled, leaving everything to the blood-stained hands of Bronstein and Gurevich. These entered into full control of the refinery and sold the stock of sugar at fabulous prices.

Such was the end of a family of nobles.

. . . . .

Alighting one day in September 1924 at the Gare St. Lazare in Paris, I tried to find a vacant taxi among the departing crowd. Every cab was taken already. I put my bag down and was preparing to wait, when a taxi drove up and put down a fare before me. I pounced on the vacant vehicle at once. To my amazement, the man at the wheel called out my name with an exclamation of surprise. Flinging out a grimy hand, he gripped my arm.

" Don't you remember me ? " he asked. " I'm Sasha Torloff."

Indeed, it was my old friend, the son of Count Torloff, who was murdered far away in Russia four years previously. Escaped with nothing but an old suit and a pair of mouldy boots, he had arrived in Poland with the coin of hope in his heart, and the joy of being at last beyond the teeth of the Soviet sharks.

Now he is earning his living as a taxi-driver with a courage that speaks well for Russia's future,

The End of a Family of Nobles

when the nightmare of Bolshevism is no more. For thousands of his fellow-countrymen are working with the same courage as he, after they had known the richest ease and comfort.

I went to his humble room, up a musty old staircase in an ancient house near the church of St. Sulpice, and saw his cousin, a lad of eighteen, who works hard in a factory by day and attends aristocratic gatherings in the evening with undiminished elegance and *savoir faire*.

Their only complaint is that some workers are hostile to them because of their breeding, blind to the noble courage of their suffering, deep-seared, youthful hearts, and still nursing the mad delusion that Soviet Russia has other to offer the majority of workers than communistic chains, famine and torrents of blood.

The family of nobles is gone, but such a noble family can never die.

Chapter V

THE ERA OF RASPUTIN

SAINT OR SINNER? Anyone who has lived in Russia long enough knows that in that semi-oriental country, one can be both at the same time. The fatal doctrine of all-forgiveness having ousted the old ascetic Christian conceptions, set holiness beyond the narrow frame of conventional morality. To sin was human nature, to forgive, man's participation in the divine. Not seven times, but seventy. This doctrine led, of course, to strange results. As fast as one offended, one forgave, as fast as one forgave, one offended. Punishment was a cruelty, an injustice, a lack of Christianity. Not to forgive was the only crime. The all-embracing Russian mind seemed to square the circle of moral sin. The Western religious sense of legality in righteousness was lacking. Anarchy seemed so natural to the Russian soul that even its religion was emptied of its binding form. While accepting the traditional teaching of the necessity of conformity to the moral law, the Russian Church seemed never to have been able to graft it on to the nihilistic Russian soul. The Russians themselves freely admit that they lack positive "character". The actions of most Russians are like a moving picture of emotions without any abiding distinction of right or wrong. Sin and you will be forgiven. Not seven times, but seventy, that is, *ad infinitum*. Conventionality, reputation, respectability, public opinion as positive forces did not exist. "We Russians", Madame Olga Novikoff declared, "never kneel to deities of that kind. We must have something solid, a religious 'categorical imperative', as the Germans say." And the only religious imperative that prevailed was that of all-forgiveness. Moral integrity, as a thing of honour every Western man desires and strives for, did not exist. There could be no distinction of persons where everything was forgiven as fast as one offended. The Western idea of righteousness, of merit in conforming to the law, had no practical value. Saints were those who were filled with this mystic all-love, all-forgiveness. Man was justified by forgiveness. No one could say of another that he was morally better than any other. No one troubled to observe the law, only to forgive. So to expect any stability, any positive force in the law, was out of the question. People went on their endless circle of offence and forgiveness from one year's end to the other. In the long run it seemed that neither offence nor forgiveness had any meaning. They were just national habits. There was none who could say: "Now this is the last time!" Such a person would have been held up to public opprobrium as an inhuman monster, a heartless being, for as every student of Russian knows in Dostoievsky's words: "The heart rules Russia".

From this it is obvious that no organism, whether of personality, the individual or the State, could save itself from disintegration. The positive law was ever being drained of its life-blood by this mental Nihilism, whether religious or political. Conscience, as Western people understand it, did not exist. That was quite natural, for no law existed which could not be broken with the expectation of entire forgiveness, seventy times a day. With the prevalence of such an anarchical, nihilistic mentality, it is not surprising that the only "categorical imperative" that was effective outside of certain highly cultured individuals, was the knout, the iron hand, force. This is well illustrated in the popular proverb: "Christ Himself would steal, if His hands weren't nailed to the cross."

Yet here again, force became impotent, because the very people employed to apply it, needed it themselves to keep them in the path of the law. In no other country of the world has there ever been such a tremendous network of agents and counter-agents, spies, counter-spies and counter-counter-spies, as there was and is in Russia. The result, however, has always been a happy-go-lucky, nichevo, lax, corrupt state of affairs, coupled with fearful iniquities and ferocious repressions. For as fast as "justice" was done, the evil cropped up again, like an everlasting, irradicable weed.

Most Russians, with a frankness that is almost breath-bereaving, relate their shortcomings, sometimes, it would appear, with morbid enjoyment. To Westerns, schooled for ages in righteousness and respectability, honour and so forth, this seems almost incredible. But there is nothing unusual in this for a Russian. He loses nothing. These "deities" were never his and never affect him. In fact, he enjoys analysing himself, as he does everything. I talk of the typical Russian, not of those very few who love their country with a Western kind of patriotism. But they are infinitesimal, and it is just they who have always proclaimed the indispensability of autocracy and the knout for keeping their fellow-countrymen in order. "Russia needs the whip" was their favourite slogan. Not only they, but all who have ruled Russia have applied it; the Tsars tempered it with happy-go-lucky mercy, the Bolshevists wield it with merciless inhumanity.

Russians like to speak for themselves. Here is the declaration of a Bolshevik : [1]

"The Russian question must be looked at from its own point of view and not from yours, for we have rejected civilization and culture. Of these we have retained nothing and we despise them in your countries, for they are qualities that are not practical. Our strength is in the fact that we have become savages again. From a humanitarian point of view, the qualities demanded by the struggle for life are brutal, coarse, base and

[1] *La Revue Universelle*, April 1923.

ugly. ... We have no word of honour, and there is no promise of ours to France, England or Germany we dream of keeping. But one will believe us, all countries will believe us, for no one knows our mentality, no one understands our soul.

"This mentality is the same as has always existed in the masses of the Russian people. The credit which was once given to Russia was based upon a misunderstanding. The Russia of the Tsar, the well-bred, well-educated Russia of the upper classes, who had in their veins 96 per cent. of foreign blood, was the screen behind which lay concealed the true Russia, which nobody, neither the foreigners nor the Russian intellectuals, knew. The screen has fallen and now the horrified world thinks it is looking at the face of the Cheka" [the Bolshevist Terror].

It was to this Russia that the upper classes themselves seemed to have succumbed. Previously they had despised it, even refusing to speak the Russian language, but since the creation of a national literature, art and "culture", they turned to it with as much fervour as they had formally held it in contempt. Till then, they had been the bearers of European civilization to Russia. Yet under this fertilization from above, the mysterious soil of the native Russian soul began to produce a fruit in accordance with its nature. A sort of intermediary class between prince and peasant came into being and grew. Its gospel was Nihilism. It was the fruit of European civilization transplanted into the steppes. It dissolved. Turguenieff noted the rise of this tide in *Fathers and Sons*. By the time of the revolution of 1905 it had swamped all classes, save a small section of patriots held up to universal execration as the " Black Hundred ". European culture became merely a gilded relic even among the haughty aristocracy.

When I wrote of my experiences of this period of Russian history in a former work, some people, ignorant of the real Russia, were fearfully shocked. I will quote, therefore, what Russians themselves have to say about their country.

Madame Vyroubova, the friend of the Empress, declares in her Memoirs : [1] " I must tell the truth, otherwise it would have been better for me never to have written. Yet to picture in anything like its true colours the decadence of Petrograd society from 1914 onward is a task from which every loyal Russian must shrink. Without a knowledge of these conditions, however, students of the Russian revolution will never be able to understand why the fabric of government slipped so easily from the feeble hands of the Provincial Government to the ruthless and bloody grasp of the Bolshevists.

" During the entire winter of 1915, when millions of Allies were giving up their lives in the cause of freedom, the aristocracy of the Russian capital was indulging in a reckless orgy of dancing, sports, dining, yes, and wining also, in spite of the

[1] *Memoirs of the Russian Court*, 1923 (Macmillan).

Emperor's edict against alcohol, spending enormous sums for gowns and jewels, and in every way ignoring the fact that the world was on fire and civilization was battling for its very life. . . . Society, when it was not otherwise amusing itself, was indulging in a new and madly exciting game of intrigue against the throne. To spread slanders about the Empress, to inflame the simple minds of workmen against the State was the most popular diversion of the aristocracy. . . . Russia, like eighteenth-century France, passed through a period of acute insanity. . . . It pervaded the Duma, the highest ranks of society, Royalty itself, all as guilty of Russia's ruin as the most bloodthirsty terrorist. . . . For years before the revolution the national spirit was in a state of decline. Few men or women cherished ideals of duty for duty's sake. Patriotism was practically extinct. Family life was weakened, and, in the last days, the morale of the whole people was lower than in almost any other country of the civilized world."

As to the bourgeoisie, Mr. Stephen Graham wrote in 1915:[1] " If once the Russian nation becomes thoroughly perverted, it will be the most treacherous, most vile, most dangerous in Europe. For the perverted Russian all is possible ; it is, indeed, his favourite maxim, that all is permitted, and by ' all ' he means all abomination, all fearful and unheard-of bestiality, all cruelty, all falsity, all debauch."

It seems a pity that some people did not read

[1] *Changing Russia*, 1915.

this in 1915. It would have spared them the trouble of being shocked when they read my experiences in 1925.

Mr. Graham sums up the Russian bourgeois as follows: " Selfish as it is possible to be, crass, heavy, ugly, unfaithful in marriage, unclean, impure, incapable apparently of understanding the good and true in their neighbours and in life— such is the Russian bourgeois."

As for the intelligentsia, who had rejected religion as a relic of susperstition and were striving for power, screaming out to the world for sympathy, their mass movement is best described by a foreign observer : [1]

" After the appearance of Artzibastcheff's novel *Sanin* in 1907, free love was propagated with a passion as never before, and numberless ' wild marriages ' were made, in which the emphasis is to be laid more on the wildness than on the marriage. Numerous intellectuals were possessed by sensual madness and vied with one another in orgiastic extravagances. The barriers between the sexes were suddenly overthrown and the natural boundaries which shame and morality have set up in the relations of the sexes were boldly ignored. Chastity ? A ridiculous atavism ! Fidelity ? A notion of the Flood-age ! A man who drove himself to his grave with excess was looked upon as a genius. A very race after sensual pleasures began, and the winner was the man who became most like a monkey. The cynical sex-

[1] Dr. Rosenburg, *Figuren der Russischen Literatur*, Munich, 1919.

communism of Artzibastcheff's book was the new gospel of the Russian intelligentsia before the war."

Those who opposed this terrible gospel were ignominiously labelled " reactionaries, Powers of Darkness, Black Hundred ". The " latest dictum of science " left them in a sad, unenviable backwater. The great tide was carrying the nation on to materialistic glory. . . .

Such was the soil on which Bolshevism spermed, itself the apotheosis of the evil forces from which it drew its life. It was there, thrusting its hideous face into one's eyes long before Lenin established it as the system of the Communist paradise.

As to religion itself, it seemed to have no connection with conscience, except when, crossing himself and bowing before the ikons, the Russian would swear that he was telling the truth when all the time he was telling a lie. Mysticism, however, abounded.

There is a poem by Alexander Blok, Russia's greatest modern poet, which gives a good picture of Russian religion :

> " To sin shamelessly, with never an end,
> To lose all count of day and night,
> And, with head athrob from drunkenness,
> To pass into the House of God.
>
> Three times to bow down to the ground,
> Seven times to sign one's self with holy cross
> And secretly to touch with heated brow
> The soiled, bespitted floor.

And placing in the plate a copper coin,
Three times, yea, seven times more on end,
To kiss the ancient ikon, poor and plain
And worn away with kissing.

Then, returning home, to cheat
Someone for that very coin,
And hiccuping, to kick away
The hungry hound from before the door.

And underneath the ikon-lamp
To drink tea, counting on the abacus,
Then, opening the cupboard,
To turn the banknotes with spittled thumb.

And on the feather bed to sink
In heavy, heavy sleep . . .
Yes, even so, my Russia,
Thou art dearer than all lands to me."[1]

Religion, therefore, was not a social convenience or moral imperative in Russia, but a well of mysticism, a sort of spiritual voluptuousness. Perhaps in this Russia was nearer eternal truth than we know. The social atmosphere, however, was obviously full of possibilities, and it was in this great abyss of anarchy and impending Bolshevism that there emerged two of the most startling figures of modern history, Gregory Rasputin and Vladimir Lenin. The former brought no new gospel. His one aim was to rescue Russia from the welter of moral evil into which the bankrupt intelligentsia and the corrupt bureaucracy had led it. His creed was the old one of self-discipline, ascetic self-denial and the wholesomeness of personal

[1] Rodina, Stikhi, 1916.

virtue. As such he was a symbol of "the Powers of Darkness," a relic of bygone "superstition" and "mental enslavement" for which the emancipated, "scientific", intelligentsia, proclaiming unfettered reason and absolute freedom from all the "mouldy traditions" of the dark past, had not only a profound contempt but a screaming, gesticulating hatred. To the haughty, autocratic aristocracy he was nothing but a moujhik, a low serf, and a dangerous one, for he advocated the strengthening of the bonds between the Orthodox Tsar and the pious peasantry by the creation of a robust element of peasant proprietors. This policy had already been attempted by the Minister, Stolypin, who had paid for it with his life. The infuriated land-owning nobles would not hear of a policy that could only be carried out at the expense of their land and power. Professor Ossendowski declares that they arranged for Stolypin's assassination by "agents provocateurs" and that they dubbed him "the slayer of the nobles".[1]

Rasputin, however, carried on his campaign fearlessly. His efforts on behalf of Christian morality and asceticism, the inner discipline and moral strength which results from restraint and self-control, stank in the nostrils of the debauched intelligentsia, whose slogan was "Everything is permitted", a slogan culled from Nietzsche. Of the good-living intellectuals, who, alas, were a dwindling company, few could face the shame of seeing any good in a mere moujhik. Their god

[1] *The Shadow of the Gloomy East.*

The Era of Rasputin

was reason, yet they failed to realize that the collective reason of an organized society was largely dependent for its proper functioning on the moral capitalism which was preached by the uneducated moujhik. Never, perhaps, has almighty reason produced such a crop of madness and inhumanity as it achieved in the land where it was hoisted on the altar. Reason itself is not a disembodied spirit floating about the universe, dissolving all things. It is chained to the past and to circumstances. For the purposes of life and society it must be taken in hand by a restraining guide. It needs a moral interpreter. Either that is performed by man's own efforts towards a moral synthesis or it is imposed upon him by some tyrant. Reason itself is not much good unless there is some other power to prevent the body that bears it from being ravaged or murdered.

It was when Rasputin failed that the tyrant Lenin came and set himself up to interpret reason to Russia, speaking *urbi et orbi* with pontifical authority and blasting all " unenlightened " men to bits with bombs and bullets, or mercilessly condemning them to death or ignominy in the halls of the Cheka. The intelligentsia cried out against him, but he would have no beating about the bush. His was the " latest dictum of science," the final word of that reason which they had applied to all things. Why hesitate, when with one stroke all men could be emancipated from their chains and the communism of reason established? And if he swept away all religion and "bourgeois" morality, it was because they had already ceased to exist as vital forces among the intelligentsia and had been condemned by their own emancipated reason as the dead wood of bygone superstition and out-of-date society. The cry that rose from the astounded Russian intelligentsia was the cry of horror of a man who sees his hideous face for the first time in a revealing mirror. Lenin merely established as a system the amorality which had so long been the ruling power before him. Perhaps that explains his heartfelt contempt of all who tried to justify "bourgeois" morality. But before this stage of development could be reached a great struggle for the old dying values was necessary. The intelligentsia should have realized that the final outcome of their negations and strivings was Bolshevism. It was not a sudden growth, something that sprung up mysteriously on the soil of Russia. They were breeding it themselves all the time. But they did not think of where their "unfettered reason" would land them. (By "unfettered", they usually meant lack of all moral "chains". Unfettered reason and unfettered morals, if there is such a thing, always went together.) They were too happy smashing down the symbols and traditions of the past. For them Rasputin was the symbol of "benighted" Russia, the Russia of the religious-minded moujhik, of ignorance and superstition. In one sense, they were right. One could not witness the futility of religious observances in Russia during their appalling decadence without wishing for something better. But the "enlightenment" they had to offer led inevitably to Nihilism, while, removed from its idealistic jargon, their only final goal was a sort of glorified materialism. They seemed to forget that man did not live by bread alone, and that what Russia needed was not a sweeping negation of its religion in the name of reason, science and the "latest dictum", but a renewal of the vivifying forces that are common to all religion. But this they could not do, for they rejected even the latent natural religion in themselves, and had established orgiastic sensuality and all spiritual negation as their rational creed. It was not a direct outburst of depravity, it was born with groans and agonies, the fruit of unfettered reason's "enlightenment" against the pitch-black, all-engulfing darkness of eternity. Russia, perhaps, has born the cross of the world in her flesh more martyr-like than one may guess. But it was a cross of her own making and her martyrdom has cost the blood of millions. Had Russians foreseen the bloody goal and the terrible misery to which their "enlightenment" was leading them, they might have altered their course. But when the dissipated aristocracy slew the man who represented the sad, lonely movement for the spiritual redemption of Russia on the old lines of Christian strength and virtue, the intelligentsia rejoiced its loudest. Rasputin was, of course, merely the symbol of their personal bugbears. To the nobles he was the symbol of the loathsome moujhik and the advocate of the peasant-proprietor policy. They wanted the peasant kept in his place and the land policy crushed. To the intelligentsia he was the symbol of Orthodoxy, religious superstition, the strengthening of which meant always the strengthening of Autocracy, of the Orthodox Tsar. They wanted the Tsar removed altogether with the Church that upheld him as "the Lord's Anointed". Both forces had their way. Rasputin was removed by the aristocrats, and almost immediately the Tsar was removed by the intelligentsia.

GREGORY RASPUTIN.

[To face p. 80.

Chapter VI

DAYS AND NIGHTS
WITH RASPUTIN

AT MY FIRST MEETING with Gregory Rasputin I was not particularly attracted to him. He had the peasant atmosphere externally, which is quite pleasant and interesting in its proper place, but seemed at first rather revolting in the vicinity of royalty. Moreover, he was a rugged fellow, huge and horselike, and it certainly gave no satisfaction to one's aesthetic sense to look at him with his oily long hair and black beard, coarse, bulging Epstein lips and horsy hands. But this ruggedness had a peculiar charm, an appeal, not to one's refining sense of beauty but to the more primitive, grosser sense of forcefulness, such as one experiences at the sight of a fine massive cart-horse after viewing the Derby winner. But it was not this coarseness that took him to the Court, though it had invaded almost every sphere of Russia. It was only after I had entered into more intimate relations with him and his entourage that I began to realize what an extraordinary, Viking type of man he was.

Moreover, one could never forget that the most dreadful depravity was attributed to him. Being the friend of so many of his friends and admirers and knowing the integrity and genuine piety of their lives, I owed it to them not to give too easy credence to the villainous stories that reached my ears, for they, too, by implication were alleged to be his accomplices. In writing of this heinous campaign against Rasputin, Madame Vyroubova, the Tsarina's friend, attributes it to " the strangely abnormal and hysterical mentality of the Russian people at that epoch . . . the madness and confusion of the Russian mind. That this madness, this unreasoning mania for the destruction of all institutions might have something to justify itself in the public mind, it was absolutely necessary to find and persecute individuals who typified, in popular imagination, the things which were so bitterly hated. Rasputin, more than any other individual in the Empire, did typify old and unpopular institutions ". As a religious supporter of Autocracy, he was hated by the Westernising intelligentsia, as a peasant he was loathed by the arrogant nobles, and as the advocate of asceticism and the discipline of the body, he was abhorred by both, whose gospel was sex anarchy and debauch. He advocated self-control for the strengthening of body and mind and the development of the soul, while his foes were already vowed to riotous living, birth-control and debauch for debauch's sake, as " the latest stage of emancipation and evolution ", " progress ". Having seen and heard so much dismissed and abolished as " prejudice ", " superstition ", " out-of-date ", one sometimes wonders where " progress " is likely to lead to. Rasputin, moujhik though he was, had something of the penetrating vision of an Old Testament prophet. He had the same keen sense of the connection between the moral health and the social life of the nation. He stood for the binding force of religious discipline against the dissolving influence of too much pseudo-science. All of which is an old story and might have been told by any dear country curate over a cup of tea. But the difference lies in the fact that it was told by Rasputin, in Russia, and in his own peculiar manner. And the end of his story was the downfall of the State and the confirmation of all the evil he had predicted.

A short while after my introduction to Rasputin, he sent me his photograph, taken as he stood beside the monument which M. Arendsen, a Danish sculptor, was executing to the memory of Alexander III. When I next saw him at the house of Countess Ignaieff, in Tsarkoe Selo, I begged him to sign it and write an inscription. At the top of the photograph he wrote the cryptic words: " Vy tam, my zdies " (you there, we here). I couldn't make out what this stood for. I realized my mystical *flaire* was rather off-scent, so I begged him to be a little more explicit. He looked at me good-humouredly and shook his head. " A faithful hound goes not twice round the yard to find his master's entrance," he said, in that slow, deep, velvet-toned voice of his. Whether he meant that it was a simple matter or that I was dull of wit I don't know. He took the pen up once more and wrote at the bottom of the photograph: " You pray there, we pray here." Then I realized that he was depicted at the tomb of the Emperor and that he was referring to the souls of the faithful departed, and their communion in prayer with the faithful on earth. He was fond of dwelling on the need for prayer and thanksgiving, which put people into a mystical communion with the spirits of the other world. On Sundays after Mass he would usually meet people in the house of some aristocratic admirer and talk to them. I remember hearing him in the drawing-room of Countess Ignaieff one Sunday. The chairs were all in their dust-hustings as was the custom except on high feast days, while the floor was bare, so there was not that creature comfort so conspicuous in English drawing-rooms. There, everyone, even Countess Heyder, who had taken her degree in philosophy, listened to his caressing, forceful voice with rapt attention. It is impossible for me to convey an adequate idea of the richness of his voice, its manly pathos, its melodious and exquisitely shaded intonations, its slow, poetic rhythm. For that, one must know what it is to hear a good Russian peasant, for it is recognized even by Russian writers that the Russian peasant in his native simplicity speaks perfect, fascinating Russian. Whereas the English or Scotch yokel speaks a jarring dialect, most Russian peasants speak purest Russian in an accent that is clean and melodious.

Rasputin declared: "To praise God, seeking nothing, like the bird singing on the green branch, that is the great affair for the Christian soul. Why does the bird build its nest, feed itself and its young, live its short life? Only that it may sing, because its song is a praise to God. It does not ask itself about life or death. It lives, praising God with its song in its bird's soul. Man must live to praise God. Life is not to eat, to drink, to dress in fine clothes. Life is to praise God, asking for nothing, giving all."

He thought that man should praise God by developing all that was best in himself. Young people should exercise their bodies to make them beautiful. "God loves a beautiful pilgrim," was his favourite saying. People should train their voices, to make them lovely so that they might praise God and God might be proud of them. If they fell in love, it was that they might give children to God and keep up the glory of God on earth. They should watch over and tend everything beautiful in their souls, their bodies, develop their talents and make the world more wonderful. But they should always be on their guard against pride and the devil. They must discipline their bodies, so that their spirit might sing to God. It did not matter if they had been wrong-doers before. He himself in his young days had been led astray by the evil one, and he was still known as "Rasputin" (the wayward).

He still kept the nickname for humility and to praise God for his coming to the knowledge of divine love. The rebellion of the flesh was the cause of all the evil in the world. It scarred the face of the earth. It was the plague of mankind, because it took all for itself, hoping to possess, whereas it grasped only the shadow of a spectre. If one praised God, one gave all, keeping nothing for one's self, thinking not of one's self. But God was pleased with this and enriched the poor giver.

I had the temerity to ask him some time after whether he thought a crow might give praise with its hideous cawing. He looked at me quite solemnly, laid his large hand on my sleeve, and said, shaking his head: "That, my friend, is not a bird of God. The crow is like the owl, a bird of ill-tidings (zlovyestchaya). Such birds will not be in the Kingdom of God."

One of the most surprising things I saw was when an old woman, bedridden with rheumatism for years, was brought to him at his house on the Gorokhovaya. It was with difficulty that she was brought in on a stretcher and placed in the middle of the crowded room. Rasputin had been having tea with his guests and was not prepared for the woman. She must have bribed her way in. When they brought the woman into the room, he rose and laid his hands on her wrinkled brow.

"Pray to Saint Xenia," he said, somewhat harshly.

The old woman's eyes welled up with tears. She held up her twisted hands.

"I prayed," she stammered, her voice broken with despair. "As a pilgrim I went. To the monastery at Kiev I went. To the saints I prayed. Nothing. Still I drag on this miserable life. Help, batiushka! help an unfortunate one!"

Rasputin, who had turned away, embarrassed, and was asking who had brought the woman in, suddenly swept away his seeming indifference, and taking the disfigured woman in his powerful arms, raised her up and kissed her brow.

For a moment she groaned with pain at the sudden movement, then seizing the cross which hung on a chain on Rasputin's breast, pressed it passionately to her lips.

"Glory to Thee, Lord, glory to Thee! Help, Merciful One, help!" she cried out.

Rasputin kissed her brow again and lifted her up from the stretcher. She clung to his strength grimly, kissing the cross and calling out for mercy. When he set her down, she surprised the whole company by standing on her feet. It was the first time she had been able to do so for twenty years or so. She was shaky, it is true, but she managed to walk across the room and kiss the ikon in the corner. Naturally, the joy and exultation that pervaded the company was unforgettable. Tears were shed abundantly and women sunk on to their knees in thanksgiving. The atmosphere was most electric. I was myself so stirred that I could hardly keep from either weeping or throbbing like the rest.

He always exercised a strange influence over

the sick and was able to cure many in a way that was said to be miraculous. The only instance I knew personally was the one I have just described, though in that case the great emotionalism of the woman and the surrounding atmosphere must have helped considerably.

For certain aspects of Rasputin I had the same experience as Madame Vyroubova, who writes: " I do not know whether or not in Western countries religion produces in the neurotic and shallow-minded a kind of emotional excitement which they mistake for faith, but in Russia there was a time when this was so. For the most part, however, it was really serious people, men and women, who went in after Mass to listen to the discourses of Rasputin. He was, as I have said, an unlettered man, but he knew the Scriptures, and his interpretations were so keen and so original that highly-educated people, even learned churchmen, liked to listen to them. In matters of faith and doctrine he could never be confused or confounded. Moreover, his sympathy and his charity were so wide and tender that he attracted women of narrow lives whose small troubles might have been dismissed as trivial by ordinary confessors. For example, many lovelorn women (men too) used to go to those morning meetings to beg his prayers on their heart's behalf. He knew that unsatisfied love is a very real trouble and he was always gentle and patient with such people, that is, if their souls were innocent. For irregular love affairs he had no patience whatever."

Days and Nights with Rasputin

I have said that Rasputin was a saint in so far as he, a poor man, stood alone in Russia in not accepting bribes. Madame Vyroubova holds similar views: " This indifference to money on the part of Rasputin was all the more conspicuous in a country where almost every hand was stretched out for reward, graft, or blackmail." Regarding the wild tales about him, she says: " I heard, I suppose, every wild tale that was told of him. But no one ever presented to the Imperial Family or to myself any evidence, any facts in support of these accusations."

And such was my own experience, too. When it became bruited that Rasputin had been thrown out of the Yar restaurant in Moscow, I went with a young Russian friend to get the details of the disgraceful scene on the spot. To my relief no one at the restaurant knew anything about the matter at all. My friend and I had an expensive meal there and when we gave the waiter a handsome tip, he became loquacious.

" The devil knows who comes here," he said. " Rasputin or any other, it is all the same to us. Here we get all sorts of phizzes, red, white, black and green. But Rasputin, that's yerunda ! (bunkum). No Rasputin here ! There was a row the other night, as you mention. That was a quarrel between two officers. One of them offered a diamond ring to the other officer's wife, or the woman he was with. She was indignant and felt insulted. They had a terrible rumpus. Swore at each other, shouted, and one of them threw a champagne bottle at the other and overturned the dinner table, together with the plates and glasses. The uproar! The gorodovoys came in and threw the man out. That's all. Of Rasputin, no word even!"

I felt very happy, because Rasputin was reported to have made such impossible remarks about the Empress that I could not feel at rest until I had investigated the report on the spot. It was a malicious tale, but alas, only one of the hundreds that were poured out every day by the diseased, fevered brains of the disloyal degenerates.

The President of the Czecho-slovak Republic, Dr. Massryk, who knew Russia well, also declared that " The nobility reeked of the moral and political degradation that surrounded the Court. They were against Rasputin not for moral or religious reasons, but for reasons of caste. . . . Russia was fated to fall and to fall through her own inner falsehood. . . . Perhaps the chief blame lies with the Russian Church and its failure to give the people moral education."

And this was because religion in Russia had little to do with morality. So that, even if Rasputin had committed moral depravities, he would not on that account have suffered any diminution in the eyes of Russia. The immorality that was attributed to him so furiously meant little as such to a people who cared nothing for morals. It was the deliberate linking of his name with the occupants of the throne and their family that counted. It had no other purpose than to destroy the prestige of Nicholas II. The campaign of calumny was fostered by the Grand Ducal cabal for their own interests and schemes, and by the revolutionary intelligentsia for the overthrow of Autocracy altogether.

Rasputin knew that men were after his blood. He had already been stabbed by a mad woman when I met him. One day, in the spring of 1916, I met Rasputin on the steps of St. Isaac's cathedral. He asked me to come and have tea with him the following day, but I told him that I was leaving early the next morning for a little trip to the wild shores of Lake Ladoga. I had a young Russian student friend who was fond of going to wild spots and living in a sort of backwood fashion. Rasputin smiled at the idea, declaring that he often longed to go back to his far-off home in Siberia and the odours of the spring in the vast forests. He wanted to come with us. At first I thought that he was just expressing a fleeting fancy, but he insisted that he was in earnest.

It was rather embarrassing for me, as Serge, my friend, was deep in the mire of revolutionary intrigues common to students at the university, and would be sure to treat Rasputin with lashing contempt and studied insult, which, I regret to admit, were very prevalent even among the highest circles owing to the terrible looseness of Russians tongues and their inborn incapacity to control their lust for talking and expressing their feelings uphill and down dale.

I rang up Rasputin and told him that if he

cared to go he must make his way there alone, as I was going with a friend who did not wish to have a third companion. Perhaps he would join us as a chance acquaintance. We were going to Olonetz on the shores of the lake and from there to a tiny hamlet about five versts northward, where Serge kept a small yacht. I told him Serge's name, so that he could be directed.

I thought I should hear no more of his sudden desire to join us. It was just a flash in the pan. About nine o'clock next evening, after a day spent in yachting on the lake and shooting in the thick forests, we moored the boat to the trunk of a tree and started to make a camp fire with which to roast the wild duck we had shot. We were far from human habitations, alone on the ridge of the slumbering forest, listening to the rapping of the woodpeckers, the cries of woodcocks, snipes, glukhari and other game and enjoying the enchanting stillness of the beautiful white night. It would never get dark. The white light would go on till the sun rose soon after midnight to set the forest afire with its flaming hues and suffuse its laughing warmth through the gleaming pallor of the lake.

Serge was tinkering the sails of the tiny yacht, while I was looking after the odorous, sizzling duck over the wood fire, when we were startled by the splash of oars and the loud, echoing voice of a peasant.

"Hoi, brothers! Like worms in the wood you hid yourselves. Glory to God! We have found them at last! Ekh! thou, little brother! We shall drink a merry little glass for this!"

The forest resounded with the peasant's fat laughter. As the boat drew nearer we were surprised to see Rasputin sitting in the stern. He waved his hand when he saw me and boomed out his familiar " Peace to the servants of God ! "

He stepped out of the boat and held out his large hand. " So we have come, little brother, to breathe with a full breast and listen to the secret voices," he said. " Here is the palace of the eternal, invisible God. Here all is quiet, bright, clean ; a godly refreshment."

Serge was muttering something unpleasant, but I took him in hand at once and told him in French that if he didn't make himself agreeable to Rasputin I would go back to the city at once. He subsided fairly willingly, for I had already impressed upon him once before that I preferred to remove my presence from that of unpleasant people if they were not prepared to remove themselves or reform. There is nothing that surprises Russians so much as this capacity to forego a man's company rather than put up with his unnecessary deficiencies and ill-humours. On that account they usually called one " unsympathetic ", " hard-hearted ", " wooden ", etc. But in the long run they knew what to expect and behaved themselves accordingly.

Rasputin shared the roast duck and the tea we brewed with water from the lake. He chatted a long while about the Empress, the Tsarevich, the ladies of the Court and mutual acquaintances.

He wanted to go down to the front to be near the men who were fighting for holy Russia, but he was distressed to know that his enemies were very strong there and put every obstacle in the way of his visiting the peasant soldiers.

He related so well his various journeys to the famous monasteries of Russia and had such a genuine tone of sincerity and a wealth of sympathy, that the sullen Serge recovered from his prejudices and took the man to his heart. Afterwards he said to me : " Such a moujhik is a rarity. One ought to have a blank gramophone record always behind him. It's a pity he isn't ordained. If he had a hermit's cell (kelya), all Russia would flock to him."

We rolled ourselves up in our blankets and gave a rug to Rasputin. He did not care to sleep at once. The white night was so clear and light that he preferred to walk about the shore of the lake.

Tired out, I soon dropped off to sleep. I was wakened some time later by the sound of singing. Looking round, I saw the figure of Rasputin standing dark against the shimmering surface of the vast lake. The white night was already melting into the glow of sunrise, the far waters beyond the shadow of the forest seeming to rise into the air on shining wings. White flashes of sheet lightning darted across the horizon like the rhythmic sweep of a giant wing. The tree-tops swayed in the light breeze with a lulling rustle, while the cries of the awakening wild fowl resounded in the hollow depths of the mossy, wayless forest. In this choir of nature, the voice of the Staretz, singing some melodious, half-melancholy hymn or psalm of old Slavonic, rose and fell like the wave of sound from a deep-toned bell. Somehow it struck me that I was listening to a wonderful old prophet of the desert singing his lamentations over the waters of Babylon. I listened attentively and concluded that he was singing the Lamentations of Jeremiah, whose voice of threatening prophecy he was fond of making his own.

I had heard so many Jeremiahs in my lifetime, that I paid no special heed to that part of his mission, though I knew his condemnation of the iniquities of his countrymen was only too well founded. Only when Russia lay prostrate, its Tsar murdered, its people slain in millions by the Bolshevists, and Petrograd was emptied of its dwellers and had become a waste place, did the full force and truth of this unlettered man's mission and prophecy come home to me. "While I am alive, the throne is safe," had been his constant plea.

.   .   .   .   .

When I came to England in December 1916, just before his assassination, I tried to put his cause before the British public, but not one newspaper would give me space, nor would any public servant listen to my version of Rasputin's real rôle. Most, alas, were convinced that Rasputin was a dangerous person and that it would help the cause of the Allies if he was forcibly removed.

The Blue Steppes

It was my previous knowledge of these views which caused me to listen with much interest to the opinion of many people in Russia after the revolution that it had been brought about with the connivance of a well-known diplomat and the Allies. If that is so, then the assassination of Rasputin at the house of Prince Felix Yusoopoff must have had the previous approval of the Allied politicians. The work was the result of the Grand Ducal cabal, and it is common knowledge that they arranged a good part of their plotting with the blessing of the Allied politicians, presumably for the better continuation of the war and the avoidance of a separate peace, rumours of which had been so long current in Russia. Rasputin never urged a separate peace, but always insisted that Germany should not be made to overthrow her own autocracy.

When I returned to England, after the Soviet reign of terror, almost my first step was to try once more to enlighten the British public about my murdered friend. Every ear seemed closed, but I succeeded in publishing a very short account of my views and knowledge of Rasputin in *John o' London*, under the title, " Rasputin as I Knew Him ". Even then I had to conform to a certain apologizing exordium at the request of the editor.

Whatever Rasputin was, he was a true lover of his country, his Tsar and his religion, the three things which " emancipated " Russia had affected to despise. Of the dark things attributed to him I have no personal knowledge and have never met anyone who has. In any case there was no one among the debauched intelligentsia who could throw the first stone. And having enjoyed his society pretty often, though holding my own views of the ways and means peculiar to Russian religious life, I give him the full benefit of the doubt and call him with his admirers, a martyr.

Chapter VII

THE HOUSE IN
THE HORSEGUARDS' ALLEY

I

BY THOSE MYSTERIOUS HANDS that weave our fortunes I was fated to enter the house in the Horseguards' Alley in Petrograd. It had nothing unusual in its outward look except a large square window overhanging the carriage archway. That, in itself, was nothing startling. It merely jutted out like a large glass eye in the flat surface of the long line of unpretentious mansions. As one turned the corner of the Horseguards' Avenue and looked down the alley, it winked at one with the gleam of daylight in its broad panes. On coming nearer, every passer-by looked up at it with wonder. From either side one saw the hairy form of a grinning monkey hunching about on his perch or swinging from a bright ring attached to the centre of the ceiling.

When I first saw it, in 1915, grinning at me with its hideous row of white teeth and red gums, it wore a white ruffle and a yellow satin jacket adorned with a black coronet. It was swinging

The House in the Horseguards' Alley

on the golden ring, its lower anatomy looking like a blue balloon. Next time I passed the window I was surprised to see the monkey in a red frill and a green satin jacket with a red coronet. Moreover, it was seated on the shoulder of an extremely beautiful woman, fondling her white neck and playing with the rich, dark tresses that hung loose down her back. It was already midday, but the beautiful woman was still clad in a yellow, bird-embroidered kimono, having evidently just come out of her morning bath. Late-rising was a common habit among the ladies of Petrograd owing to their fondness for night life. I found the woman so royally beautiful— she seemed to have stepped out of a Rubens picture — that the house which I had first distinguished as the house with the winking window, and then the house with the grinning monkey, became at last the house with the Rubens beauty. I wanted to know more about her.

Luckily it did not take me long to find out. Her next-door neighbour was Count Fredericks, the aged, affable Minister of the Imperial Court. He was interested in some translations I had made from Pushkin, Lermontov, and other Russian poets, and had invited me to lunch. We were just a few at table, including M. Derfeiden, a young officer whose sister danced at the palace of Prince Yusoopov on the night of Rasputin's murder, and Count Kleinmichel, a man I had known in Kharkov.

In his rather sombre dining-room, with its

dull pictures of still life on the panelled walls and an old English clock whose crazy chimes went off every ten minutes, Count Fredericks entertained his guests with tasty riabchiks and still tastier talk about the Court. He was a man of the old school (his delightfully undulous moustaches advertised the fact) and strongly disapproved of the mysticism that had invaded the Imperial family. Intensely German in feelings and outlook, he detested the presence of Rasputin at the Court, though his stern sense of duty and honour forbade him to give credence to the lurid tales which were everywhere in circulation. He confined himself to the ordinary small talk of the Court camarilla, relating trivial, harmless incidents about Madame Vyroubova and the Empress's ladies-in-waiting, their mutual antagonisms and feline sallies, about Rasputin's prophecies and visions, and what certain irate grand dukes had sworn to do in order to get rid of the pious peasant.

In the midst of such a stream of interesting talk, it was no easy task for me to lead up to the subject of the beautiful neighbour. It was not until the conversation had veered round to the gruesome subject of Princess Dolgorouki's skeleton that I found the chance good for a general discussion of the drawing-room hobbies of the Russian aristocracy. I remembered entering the drawing-room of Princess Dolgorouki's house on the English Quay and being startled by a human skeleton standing up stark and ghastly just behind the gilt screen by the door. It was the first thing

COUNT FREDERICKS, MINISTER OF THE IMPERIAL COURT.

[To face p. 100.

that struck one's gaze before one advanced to greet its beautiful and gifted owner.

Count Fredericks, though bordering on the eighties, could still twinkle a merry eye, carry his wine like a soldier, and turn a tale with the art of a past-master. A few days previously, it appeared, he had assisted the Emperor in distributing some war medals for deeds of valour. There had been a great concourse of drums and trumpets and several staff officers, heady with pride of position and the cut of their trousers, had received the Cross of St. George. Among them was a young Count Elston, whose elegance and arrogance matched his careful avoidance of danger in the trenches and his contempt for all risks on the matrimonial front. He had already, at the age of twenty-five, cheated three fellow-officers of their wives and married them one after the other. As the law permitted no more than three divorces, he was now obliged to win laurels on the military front instead of winning other men's wives, a practice that was almost universal amongst the educated classes of Russia. So he applied in the usual indirect manner through an uncle for the medal of St. George. Having got it, he asked for leave to return to Petrograd so that he might display his new glory. On the night of his arrival, he went to a large party given at Princess Dolgorouki's house. His pride and arrogance knew no bounds. His loud voice and jingling spurs kept everyone aware of him. During the evening he had occasion to go out to the cloakroom. His jingling spurs were heard retreating down the corridor. Suddenly a terrible shriek rent the atmosphere. Footmen and visitors rushed forward and discovered the haughty count lying white and prostrate on the floor. Before him stood the open door of a cupboard, in the dark hole of which shone the white skeleton of a man.

They brought him to with a little cold water. It was then explained that Princess Dolgorouki had decided to do away with the skeleton as an ornament of her drawing-room and had stowed it away in the cupboard near the cloakroom. The valorous count, wearing his shining new order, had opened the wrong door by mistake.

When Count Fredericks had finished relating this story, I found it opportune to ask who was the beautiful neighbour whose chief window adornment seemed to be a grinning monkey.

Count Fredericks burst into a merry chuckle. An old man's chuckle has the flavour of old vintage. He lifted both his hands and drew out his long moustaches with gentle caressings.

" Here's a fine young fellow ! " he exclaimed. " One eye on the poets and the other on the beauties of the natural creation. Taste . . . exquisite, as you see, gentlemen. When I was young and handsome, I was just as keen. And if in those days I had seen such a beauty as one sees every morning in the overhanging window next door, fondling that monstrous monkey, I should have known my career. Well, I'm not too old to take an interest in her even now. One can't live long next door to a monkey and a beauty without wanting to know a little of their history. I can tell you, gentlemen, that I soon took steps to find out."

"Who is she?" the men asked eagerly. "A demi-mondaine?"

Count Fredericks held up his hands and waved them downwards as though to allay such unsettling thoughts.

"By no means!" he declared. "A most respectable woman, daughter of a merchant, honorary citizen of the town of St. Petersburg. (He always spoke of the town by its historic name.) She was married at nineteen to a penniless man in the Foreign Office, divorced him a few years later and took up nursing when the war broke out. Then she made the acquaintance of Vadimsky, the proprietor of the *Petrograd Chronicle*, who was on his last legs with consumption. She nursed him devotedly till he died after making her his wife and leaving her a tremendous fortune. His newspaper sold like hot cakes since the outbreak of war. Since his death she still runs the hospital for wounded soldiers which he had opened on the top floor of the house and where she first entered his life as a war-nurse. He died about three months ago. About a month later she installed the monkey and by way of consolation sews new coats and frills for it every day. But there are other developments on the way. Now that she has inherited the Vadimsky fortune, she has a host of suitors, some of them with coronets.

She turns them all away with a weary sigh and embroiders a new coronet on the monkey's coat for each noble offer she declines."

"Is she satisfied with her bourgeois station?" Count Kleinmichel asked.

Count Fredericks chuckled in the manner familiar to those who knew him. He never looked upon courtly gravity as being anything more than a part of court dress. He always seemed to thank God for laughter.

"Is any woman satisfied with her station?" he asked. "Was Eve? We can wait and watch. It isn't because there's no apple on the tree. In fact there are too many. But most of them are far too small. Madame Vadimsky declares she will only marry for love. Very well! a lovely ideal! But some people say the Grand Duke S—— has set his eye at the lovely idealist. Marriage would be rather a difficulty. The Grand Duke would have to live abroad if he married her. Gossips hint that the Grand Duke has too much ambition at home to risk life with love abroad. But, as I said before, Madame Vadimsky is a most respectable woman. She is testing the depth of the Grand Duke's love before she comes to a decision."

II

A few days later I had occasion to visit the Prince of Oldenburg, who was connected with the Red Cross. While waiting in the ante-chamber of the large mansion next to the British Embassy,

The House in the Horseguards' Alley

I was engaged in conversation with one of the secretaries. Though he wore an officer's brown uniform and sundry ribbons, he was so puny that he seemed little more than an appendage to his ferocious black beard. His conversation and manner, however, were pleasant. As Count de Luze, his name was already familiar to me, several remarkable monuments having been erected by his father.

It never struck me at the time that he could have any connection with the house in the Horseguards' Alley. But the world is very narrow and life is full of surprises. He had taken a kind interest in my efforts to be useful in Russia during the war. I had been rejected for the army on account of my sight, but was able to make use of my knowledge of European languages, including Russian. My appeals to the British Embassy and the British War Office had all led to the receipt of the usual printed form of regrets. So in despair I had turned once more to the Russians. I was given some work interpreting and translating for prisoners of war. Count de Luze immediately inquired where I was going to put up in Petrograd. When I told him that I would like to find a small flat, he told me of a very nice one at the rear of a house he visited in the Horseguards' Alley. It was very convenient and belonged to a most charming woman.

"Does she keep a monkey?" I asked, thinking of the only woman I had noticed in the houses of the alley.

"She does so," he replied. "I suppose you've seen it in the window. I'll ring up and find out whether she can see you."

A short while after I was in the room with the grinning monkey, talking to its beautiful mistress.

In spite of her stateliness and perfection of mould, she carried with her an atmosphere of weariness. Almost every sentence she pronounced was followed by the fall of her breast and a faint sigh. When she came back from showing me the charms of Petrushka, the monkey, she leant her form against the queue of the grand piano and with a dreamy look in her large, dark eyes told me that life was a grey illusion we should learn to embroider with love. I saw on a chair near by the grey satin coat she had just been embroidering with a coronet for the monkey.

With her arms resting along the lid of the piano, she discoursed wearily on life in a voice that had a soft accent of sadness. She asked me whether the English knew what "toska"[1] was, and the red rose she wore in her opulent bosom shed its petals on to the piano at her sigh.

I feared to suggest that it could be cured with fresh air and exercise, for so many Russians hug their weariness of life as though it were a peculiar richness of soul. Moreover, I began to fear the dreamy look in the beautiful woman's eyes. Somehow I got out of my embarrassment by insinuating that I would like to see the flat.

She kindly offered to show it to me herself

[1] Weariness.

and led me down winding corridors till we appeared before windows overlooking the courtyard. The flat was well furnished and bright, with a separate entrance leading down into the courtyard.

Having described its charms to me, Madame Vadimsky sank down on to the huge divan with a sigh.

"I hope you will come and live here," she said. "I am sure we shall be great friends. It is quite like a separate dwelling, but the corridor I brought you through is always an open invitation for you to visit me whenever you please. You will come, won't you?"

Her eagerness rather startled me, but she quickly went on to explain.

"I live in this enormous house with my unmarried sister and a young son by my first husband. There is a hospital on the top floor, but nursing and the officers have become so tiresome. I just leave it to the care of the paid nurses. The ground floor I have let to my sister. She is also a widow, but soon she will marry the doctor who attends the wounded upstairs. I want you very much to take this flat. You will do me a great service. I don't wish to let it really. It is convenient for putting up relations. But there is one relation of my late husband who would give half his fortune to get a foot in the house. Perhaps I may tell you more about it later on. There are complications since my husband died. If you come, you will prevent a misfortune. You will not want to stay on permanently, but we can be quite friendly, as though you were my guest and I was doing a patriotic turn to an Englishman in Russia during the war."

She sighed deeply. A little while later I agreed to make the flat my temporary abode.

When I arrived next day with my luggage, I found a bunch of exquisite white chrysanthemums in a vase on the writing-table. A bottle of eau-de-cologne and boxes of expensive French powders stood on the dressing-table. A heap of French books lay on the small table by the side of the bed. There was that Huysman's horror, *La-bas*, together with the Queen of Navarre's literary productions and a fearful book dealing with Giles de Rais and the terrors of the Middle Ages.

It was somehow forced upon me that all this mound of horror was French, and I wondered why it was that the splendid Gallic nation should seem to provide the world with so much frightfulness. As I turned the books over, I thought of Carducci's poem:

> " Una bieca druidica visione
> Su gli spiriti cala e li tormenta.
> Da le torri papali d'Avignone
> Turbine di furor torbido venta."

What connection with the Celtic ferocity lurking in the blood of France had Madame Vadimsky? Her spirit seemed to me too tired to find even a stir at the druidic horrors that rose from time to time in France. The house in the Horseguards' Alley became yet more mysterious to me since I came under its roof. With such lavish provision for my physical beauty and the adornment of my soul, I really began to wonder where on earth I was going to. Had I entered the wrong house?

Feeling somewhat disquietened, I looked out of the window into the courtyard. Some men were busy stacking wood for the winter. From a large door next the open garage came the mooing of a cow. The windows on all sides of this mansion courtyard were neat and tranquil. Pigeons were billing and cooing on the sills, while from somewhere in the lower flat came the sound of Schumann's " Carnival " played on a piano. A few moments later I saw the car of Count de Luze being parked by the chauffeur. I concluded that the Count had just arrived. Wishing to have a chat with him, I went along the corridor and entered Madame Vadimsky's apartment. Just before I got to the entrance hall, I heard a voice and stopped for a moment, thinking visitors might be arriving. I looked into the hall and saw Count de Luze on his knees before the bathroom door. He was carrying on a sort of verbal serenade while Madame Vadimsky took her morning bath.

" My sunlit one ! " I heard him orate in a clear, well-modulated, rather emotional voice. " Whatever happens, whatever you choose to do, my one great joy is to throw myself down at your feet. I am yours for ever. Nothing gleams to me in life except to kneel at your feet and hold your hand."

At this I discreetly fled whence I had come, taking with me the ineffaceable picture of the little, black-bearded man kneeling at the bathroom door. The house seemed to me more mysterious than ever.

On my way back, I ran into Onofry, one of the menservants. I had already rewarded him well for looking after my belongings, so he was anxiously communicative.

"To-day," he said, "we are all greatly excited. A message has arrived that the Grand Duke S—— will call on Madame after lunch. Count de Luze got to know, so he has arrived to forestall the Grand Duke. They are both madly in love with Madame. Everybody is."

III

I was not at home when the Grand Duke arrived. That his visit was in some way a success was revealed to me when I came home by the excited atmosphere which filled the whole house. Madame Vadimsky seemed to have cheered up considerably, her eyes, usually so love-lorn, sparkling with a new interest. So great must have been the excitement which the Grand Duke S—— had stirred in her weary bosom that she came herself to my flat to break the news. The Grand Duke had invited her to dinner at the Bear Restaurant. He would have liked to take her to the Marine Opera House before going to the restaurant, but it would be inconvenient for the present to give people occasion to talk.

I dared not ask whether the long expected

proposal of marriage and flight abroad had taken place. I was not supposed to know anything of Count Fredericks's gossip. But I realized that some step forward had been taken. The precious orchid on her quivering bosom told me so. The Grand Duke S——, whose taste for these rare flowers was well known, had surely placed it there.

All, however, did not seem to go quite well. There was just a little speck on the horizon. Madame Vadimsky had discovered that Count de Luze had also booked a room at the Bear for the evening. In fact, she had accepted to accompany him to the Opera. She thought such an arrangement would both satisfy the Count, who, as she said with a shrug and a grimace, " pestered her " (pristaet), and satisfy the Grand Duke's wish to avoid gossip. She was, of course, treating all her household for the evening. Her brother, younger sister and widowed sister, who lived with her, would all join the Count's party at the Opera and revel with him at the Bear. She would like me to share the evening with the rest of the household. For the Bear, she had invited several well-known poets and artists. As wife of the proprietor of one of Petrograd's leading newspapers, she had always protected and encouraged budding genius. She had made her salon a meeting-place for the talents, always bringing together the artist and the editor.

She would, however, be glad if I would help to keep Count de Luze cheerful. He was inclined to look on the tragic side of things. She did not wish to offend him in any way, but she suspected he did not quite like her having accepted the Grand Duke's invitation. He was stupid to be jealous. Perhaps I could try to impress upon him that it was merely a high honour no woman could be reasonably expected to decline. Women were all made to ornament society, were they not? She would be very grateful if I accepted to join the party at the Opera and the Bear.

Of course, I went, thinking myself lucky for the chance of meeting so many of Russia's literary and artistic " stars ". There was Leonid Andreyev, mixing his eschatological gloom with sudden outbursts of uncontrollable hilarity and coarse wit. Alexander Blok, tall, fair and handsome, the most modest poet I have ever met, shed his melancholy after the second glass of champagne and composed verses on the spot, to the great delight of the company. They appeared next day in Madame Vadimsky's *Petrograd Chronicle*, a doleful hymn to dead, erotic madness. Everyone seemed to brighten up under the influence of the wines and songs. Only Count de Luze, his hand perpetually tugging at his black beard, seemed to be on tenterhooks. He danced in and out of the long, gilded room as though he could never quite make up his mind which room he ought to be in. I once went along the corridor and saw him hunching his little body outside a door and holding his hand like a trumpet to his ear. He hurried away at the sound of footsteps and disappeared into a cloakroom. As I passed the door I heard the

The House in the Horseguards' Alley

loud gruff voice peculiar to the big Romanoff men. What exactly happened at Madame Vadimsky's evening with the Grand Duke S—— I cannot say. I only know that the rivalry between the two men seemed to grow more and more acute.

Having made arrangements to take my meals at Madame Vadimsky's table, I was soon given a clearer view of the exact state of things in the household.

Every morning Count de Luze appeared for lunch. He usually arrived when Madame Vadimsky was just taking her morning bath before coming out to lunch. His form was often dimly discerned in the shadowy hall, crouching before the bathroom door, while he uttered his devotions to the invisible beauty. I often wondered how a man could behave in such a strange manner, but knew that in Russia no one ever took it for merit to hide one's feelings or not to express them in high-flown language. In fact, Russians in their daily use are both the coarsest and the most literary talkers of the world. Most Russians know, but are never bound, by what is known as good form.

As for the Grand Duke S——, his attentions continued assiduous and tender. He usually arrived in the afternoon about teatime, having first sent a commissionaire with a bouquet of costly flowers. Tea was always served separately for the couple, in Madame Vadimsky's Rococo boudoir.

Sometimes Madame Vadimsky would accompany

the Grand Duke to a cabaret or restaurant. Other evenings she would devote to Count de Luze. Thus things went on for about three weeks. The beautiful woman seemed to float bodily and spiritually between the two men. At times her face was lit with hope, at times with weary indifference, almost despair. And all the while the little, black-bearded man was urging her on his knees to marry him, while the huge Romanoff spoke his mind in flowers. The rest of his intentions were not disclosed to me.

Chapter VIII

THE HOUSE IN
THE HORSEGUARDS' ALLEY—(continued)

I

ONE DAY events at the house in the Horseguards' Alley were suddenly precipitated by the explosion of a moral bombshell. I came across to breakfast in the dining-room of Madame Vadimsky's flat and found the whole household assembled in various attires and a single mind. Madame Vadimsky herself was dressed in the bird-covered kimono in which she had first appeared to my eyes.

"The rogue! the ne'er-do-well!" she repeated, while the rest of the family joined in a sort of imitative chorus.

"It is just as I expected!" she said, turning to me as I entered the room. "He has put us into the galosh!" Which is the Russian expression for "We are in the soup!"

Who was this awful "He", I wondered? The Grand Duke? Count de Luze? All the family saw the questioning look of ignorance and surprise in my face and rushed to settle their discomforts on me, describing in excited tones all the magnitude of the evil that had been perpetrated on them by " that ne'er-do-well ".

Why the whole family should have shown such fearful alarm, I couldn't understand. From what I was told I gathered that the victim of the ne'er-do-well's attack was Madame Vadimsky alone. But, somehow, the brothers and sisters and various relations whom she had taken to live with her since she inherited the dead husband's fortune, all seemed to take the affair just as much to heart. When I had succeeded in fighting my way through a great bombardment of expletives and denunciations, I felt as ready as the rest for a taste of breakfast. While this was being served, Madame Vadimsky, assisted by the noisy punctuations of the family chorus, told me the story.

She sat at the head of the table by the shining, hissing samovar, her face still flushed with the surge of dreams and the morning's dark surprise. On the fine lace camisole that peeped through the opening of her kimono lay a quivering orchid.

" N'est-ce pas, Monsieur ? " she said, never, even in her obvious excitement, losing the languor of her voice, which seemed only to deepen. " N'est-ce pas que c'est le comble de l'insolence ? I must tell you that my late husband was a very giddy fellow. I don't know what sort of life he led till I met him, nor do I care. All that is of the past. I came to nurse him here after I had served in his hospital for the wounded upstairs for over a year. I nursed him devotedly, sparing nothing of myself, for over three months. It was too late. He died. But before he died, he declared he wished to make me his wife in order to show his gratitude for what I had tried to do for him. He said he wished me to enjoy all the good things he possessed. We were married just three days before his death. He had no relations except the old aunt who lives on the ground floor. She is half mad and may be carried off by a stroke any day. She is very strange in her ways and speech. She says she knows the whereabouts of a will which leaves half the property to her and the other half to Peter, the boy of twenty-two, whom you saw here the other day. He is a dreadful ne'er-do-well. He is the cause of all this trouble. My late husband was never married before he was married to me, but he had a child by his washerwoman. Peter was that child. My husband had him brought up at a gymnasium (secondary school) and pensioned the washerwoman off, on condition she lived in her native village and never came to town. After he died the old aunt declared that she had many years ago persuaded her nephew to adopt his son legally. We all thought she was raving, as she often does when she's on the verge of a new mental attack. But Peter heard what she said and without saying anything to me made inquiries at the Ministry of Justice. Although he was here the other day drinking tea and behaving as though he was the best of friends, accepting the big allowance I made him out of the estate, he sent me this morning a terrible letter. It was full of threats, saying that he would have me turned out of the house, that I had only married his father for the sake of the money, that he was lawful heir and had been legally adopted by his own father. He called me an interloper who had come in at the last moment to deprive him of his lawful rights. He had his father's blood in his veins, whereas I had never been Madame Vadimsky except by the will of a dying man. What do you think? Isn't this the height of insolence? Is he not a wicked ne'er-do-well?"

" Ne'er-do-well! Oojhusssny nyegodjai! " (horrible ne'er-do-well) chorused the entire household with terrific emphasis.

I condoned with Madame Vadimsky to the best of my power. It was, indeed, a dreadful blow to her at the very moment when her hopes stood high in the direction of the Grand Duke. As for penniless Count de Luze, she must have realized that in spite of his deep affection he would soon fade away from her life when she ceased to be the rich widow.

I remembered having seen Peter a few days before. He had come to tea, bringing with him a couple of young men friends of the race-course type. I was in the dining-room when he arrived and was surprised to hear someone making " popping " noises with his mouth, shouting snatches of popular songs and laughing in a hideous manner. I went into the beautiful Rococo drawing-room and saw a young man with outstanding ears and red, sensuous lips. He was enjoying the delight of poking his finger into his mouth and bringing it out with a pop, after which elegance he broke into riotous laughter. With his two companions he kept jumping about the room, sitting straddling across the chairs and pretending to ride a horse, slapping the maidservants and pinching their arms, making cat-calls, etc.

"This is my late husband's adopted son!" Madame Vadimsky said, as she introduced him. At that moment he did not know he had been legally adopted. I recognized at once the type of young man turned out by the State secondary schools. It was to avoid the contamination of the public schools that most families of the aristocracy had their sons educated at home and would send them to no institution except the Lyceum or the Law School, which were highly privileged. Yet the first step of the Kerensky Government was to "democratize" them in the name of equality!

"This wretched ne'er-do-well", Madame Vadimsky went on, "has leagued himself with the old mad aunt. Together they will do all in their power to oust me from the house and from the possession of my husband's fortune. By law I am entitled to the widow's third if no will is found. Even in that case, the ne'er-do-well declares he will insist on the newspaper being sold. It would be difficult to find such a good investment, 30 per cent. It would go for a trifle as things always do when families quarrel. In any case, it would mean long and costly litigation. I foresee all my share being swallowed up by the lawyers. Anyhow, he declares that the old mad aunt knows the whereabouts of a will in which M. Vadimsky left the estate in equal shares between them with a request to his son to make a suitable provision for me. A suitable provision!"

She waved her hand downwards with a gesture of contempt. The whole company of relations seated round the long breakfast table shuddered with horror and broke into loud execrations and protests.

"How can *he*, a washerwoman's son, know what a suitable provision means?" she asked, lifting her eyebrows and shoulders.

"Just listen to what he considers suitable!"

She unfolded the long letter she held in her hand and began to read:

"Though old Aunt Claudia is considered by you and your people to be half mad, she is quite normal. Anyhow, she has lucid intervals except when she is suffering from indigestion. We all know that your people, especially Alexander Petrovich, your cousin, have tried to get her certified as mad and shut up in a madhouse. That would suit your purpose admirably, we know. But there are smarter men in the world than any your damned family can produce. You've reckoned without me, for one thing. I intend to take Aunt Claudia out of your keeping. She will be well looked after in the house I have bought at Gatchina.

She is not so mad as you think. She was always a clever woman and looked after my deceased father's business while he was having a merry time [the phrase was more idiomatic, but I have softened the expressions of the entire reading]. She saw to it that I was legally adopted and she declares she also saw to it that I was provided for as a blood relation should be in the will she got my father to draw up when she saw how you were nursing the poor, dying man so devotedly, so affectionately, wearing your body out for his sake, angel ! "

" Kakoe nakhalstvo ! " (what impudence !) shouted the family chorus, bursting into so loud an explosion of wrath that it was some time before the spirits were quietened and the reading could continue.

"She had her wits about her for all you thought she was tottering on the verge of insanity. Anyhow, she saw to it that while you nursed my dear, deceased father you didn't nurse his fortune too. One day when you were out of the way—God knows she had to watch like a cat to seize the opportunity. You were always devoting yourself so unsparingly, taking sandwiches at the poor man's bedside so as not to leave him even for meals.— One day, I say, when you had to stay outside more than usual, old Aunt Claudia got my dear, deceased father to make a short will for my sake. It was all done in a few minutes. She gave him a fountain-pen and he wrote it with his poor, trembling, dying hands on the back of a holy picture of the Virgin of Kazan. She had to hide it away pretty sharp because your angelic footsteps sounded in the corridor. The excitement was so great that she went off soon after into one of her fits, and ever since she came to, she has been trying to remember where she hid the holy picture with my dear, deceased father's last will. She knows, however, what the terms of the will are. The estate was left between me and her, which is quite natural since we are the only blood relations, while you only became his wife by the gasp of a dying man. You ought to think yourself lucky you were even mentioned in the will. I was requested by my dear father to make a suitable provision for you. Of course, since you were

The Blue Steppes

only a petty chinovnik's wife before you took up nursing, you ought to be glad to have a sum that will keep you handsomely in a three-roomed flat, drawing-room, dining-room and bedroom, you can use the public baths like the rest of us, one of your devoted relations would no doubt be willing to act as a domestic for you. I suppose so, at least, since they now fill my dear father's mansion. You would have enough for two new dresses a year, one at Easter and one at the Falling Asleep of the Virgin."—[August 15th.]

Madame Vadimsky broke off at this point and looked before her speechless.

I administered what consolation I could, knowing the heart of the eternal Eve.

"I suppose they will both be black (she read on). Your devotion will never consent to wear any other colour, nor will it permit you to enjoy any such luxuries as automobiles, theatres, cabarets and expensive food. Your sorrow will be too deep and widowly to allow you even to dream of such frivolities.

"Meanwhile I have taken steps with the lawyers, who have taken old Aunt Claudia's testimony and written to the administration board of the *Petrograd Chronicle*. You will be allowed to draw only one-third of the receipts for the present. For so much even you must hold yourself grateful to
 "Your devoted stepson,
  "PETER NIKOLAICH VADIMSKY."

When she folded up the letter and was silent, a deep sigh rose from her breast and a glistening tear trickled down her cheek.

"It is hard," she said, brushing the tear away with a little powder puff she took from her satin bag. "See what people there are in the world. Life is one long martyrdom of suffering. When nature fails to make us unhappy, it is man who does his best."

The House in the Horseguards' Alley

After which pessimistic remark she rose wearily and went into the drawing-room, calling out lovingly, though wearily, to Petrushka in the bay window.

II

I was copying Peter's letter in my "Book of Curiosities", a sort of scrapbook I had long been keeping at the suggestion of Madame Olga Novikoff, who had once called "The Book of Nonsense", when Onofry, the manservant, entered. I had begged Madame Vadimsky to let me copy the letter in my book along with other strange incidents of my sojourn in Russia. She had been delighted to have the enormity registered in black and white in an impartial log-book, but for some reason had just sent Onofry to ask for the return of the original.

It was about five o'clock. The Grand Duke S—— must have surely arrived for his afternoon visit. Indeed, I was certain of it. A small sprig of maiden-hair fern was caught in one of the brass buttons of the manservant's coat about the middle of the body. Paid servants, I have always noticed, treat the most exquisite bouquet with the same indifference as a tray of crockery, whereas the ardour of the lover alone raises it to the level of the heart. At least, such was my experience in Russia, where the presentation of flowers by ardent lovers was as diffuse and elegant a practice as the giving of costly jewels.

The Blue Steppes

I don't know what happened at that visit of the Grand Duke S——. No doubt he was informed of Peter Vadimsky's nefarious intentions regarding the disputed estate. For some days afterwards, Madame Vadimsky seemed to go about in a state of glass-eyed torpor, sighing heavily at any remark addressed to her and wearing her kimono till late in the evening, when it was time to dress for the theatre. Consolation must have been sedulously offered to her both by the Grand Duke S—— and Count de Luze. The former arrived every afternoon at his usual hour, varying his tribute of flowers with gems and objects of art from Fabergé, the Court jeweller, and further, escorting the beautiful widow to cabarets, ballets and restaurants. As if to make up for lost ground, Count de Luze came to lunch every day, faithfully prefacing his attendance at the table with that dreadful serenade at the bathroom door. The intonations of his voice seemed to become on those occasions, whenever I happened to hear him, almost woe-begone.

It would be difficult for me to describe adequately the moods, manners and actions of Russians in their own country. The Anglo-Saxon mind is so far removed from what obtained in Russia that I have always had extreme difficulty in getting it to understand. In fact, it can never " understand ", since it is so positively attached to what it calls its own " common sense ", whereas the Russian soul is essentially negative in its relation to convention, morality, or any " prejudice " of tradition. As for reason, who can tell us where it is? Russians will prove that there is no argument which reason can put up which reason will not overthrow. And what authority is there to tell us what is reason? For any group of men to impose their view is "tyranny, prejudice", especially to the Russian who passionately desires to find a reason in life, only to find himself baffled by the dark mystery of eternity and extinction. Russia, perhaps, has shown us like a martyr how terrible are the tortures of the dark gulf into which reason alone must lead us. In this lies the tragedy of the Russian intelligentsia. It should claim less our contempt than our pity and sympathy, since its sufferings would be our own if we could feel as intensely. This we do not, because we shun intense feeling, whereas the cult of feeling was the pride of Dostoievsky's Russia. "The heart reigns in Russia" was that great writer's slogan. No one, therefore, should be surprised at Count de Luze's public outpourings, nor at any other unconventional manifestations, declarations, confessions, revelations, or disregard for public opinion. Nobody in Russia ever dreamed of regarding public opinion. There was no standard. As for expression, however, it was the national occupation. The mighty Empire of the Tsars was drowned in a sea of talk. No one seemed to realize that a little reticence is a godly thing.

So I thought very often when I was obliged to overhear the amorous disquisitions of Count de Luze at the bathroom door. Perhaps it was this

The Blue Steppes

renewal of the rivals' ardours that threw Madame Vadimsky into such a lamentable state of torpor and indecision. Coupled with the treacherous stroke of Peter Vadimsky which seemed to take the ground from beneath her feet, the lovers' insistence must have bewildered her. Even Petrushka was allowed to wear the same coat for more than three days running.

On the other hand, the members of her family were roused to active vigilance. One of them, Stepan Ivanich Piatko, a shapeless, bloated cousin of middle age, suddenly developed a whirlwind of energy. Previously he had merely divided his lethargic, flabby life between detective novels, eating, and the Russian baths. He used to rise about eleven, spend an hour at breakfast, filling his glass of tea about a dozen times at the samovar and talking with other members of the family chiefly on the future paradise of Socialism, take a ten minutes' walk to the library to change his novel, come in to lunch at half-past twelve, remain talking and eating rusks after lunch till about half-past two, retire for a few minutes while the table was cleared for tea at three, return to the table for the samovar, tea, talk and eating till about half-past four, then take his novel and go to the baths, where he would talk for another hour, sitting on the wooden shelves of the steaming chamber in a state of nature, retire to the reclining cubicle and devour the detective novel till dinner-time, after which he would remain talking and drinking tea by the samovar till it was time to go to a cabaret and night life. Such a life was typical of thousands. Only among the peasants and workers the talking was usually assisted by chewing sunflower seeds and spitting out the husks.

Since the receipt of Peter Vadimsky's letter, Stepan Piatko shed his old habits and woke to an aim in life. He rose early, as early even as mad Aunt Claudia, who lived in the flat on the ground floor, and was heard droning her prayers at five every morning. He somehow conceived a great affection for this poor old woman, who was really no relation of his. Wherever she went, he followed, offering her his help and sympathy, writing her letters and screening her from the hard blows of life.

Once I was just entering my flat by the coachway when I was surprised to see Stepan Piatko carrying some rugs out of Aunt Claudia's front door, which was under the coachway arch, and placing them in the motor-car. It was about five o'clock, the time when the Grand Duke S—— usually arrived and Piatko went to the baths. He had evidently given up that habit. As he spread out the rugs in the car, he carried on an address in a loud voice with someone inside Aunt Claudia's door.

"Leave that to me, Tiotooshka (little aunt)," I heard him say. "We shall arrange everything so that you may have a cosy time. You have never been understood really. People are heartless. Like animals, they bark at everyone that doesn't wear the same skin. Rely on me. I will be your prop. You will have nothing to fear as long as I am alive to stand by you. Come, auntie dearie, get into the little car-rie. You are safe with me."

It is impossible in English to convey the endearing sense of this big man's intonation and diminutives. Even Russian plays translated into English fall as flat as pancakes, because no English can interpret the voluminous ups and downs of the Russian intonation, the richness of its polysyllabic words, the intense feeling of its diminutives and moods.

The tottering woman, who, in fact, was little over fifty, got into the car and was solicitously covered with the rugs by Stepan Piatko, who took the seat beside her and ordered the chauffeur to drive to the Islands, a favourite spot for afternoon excursions on the Gulf of Finland.

When they returned in the evening it was to announce that Stepan Piatko had induced Aunt Claudia to pay a visit to a miraculous ikon of the Mother of God somewhere along the Schlusselberg Chausée, in the hope that her infirmity might be cured by heavenly intervention.

The announcement must have caused a stir in the household, for Onofry came to my flat with some hot water just before dinner and was bursting with news. He had had a lucky day, he said. The Grand Duke S—— had been in a generous mood and had rewarded him with a "pink 'un," (a ten-rouble note). Furthermore, Stepan Piatko had shown unmistakable signs of being a nobleman, having for the first time since his arrival in the house given him, Onofry, a tip. That was because Stepan Piatko had been to pray before the ikon and was expecting it to be brought to the house that evening.

" What ikon is it ? " I asked.

" The Schlusselberg Ikon, sir," he replied. " It has a great reputation. People go to it in pilgrimage from all over Russia. It is a wonder-working ikon. Lord, sir, I remember the days when it was only a poor little ikon on the side of a crumbling brick wall. I used to play in the field near it when I was a boy. It is near my village. I never thought it would become a wonder-worker. Praise to God ! She (the ikon) has lived till glory, the blissful one."

He crossed himself and bowed before the ikon in the corner of the room.

" It was all through a miracle," he went on. " No one ever came to the old church. It was falling into ruins. God doesn't like this place, the old people said. The pope was starving, his cassock in rags. The people were all leaving the village for the factories, for the town. How could he live, the poor one? The popadyà (pope's wife) prayed before the ikon. 'Give, intercessor ! ' she said. 'Grant help. We are beaten down with misery. We starve. Grant us to keep thy image bright, to praise thee, Mother of God.' The popadyà prayed, shed bitter tears, wiped her eyes and went into the izba. The pope was sitting under the stove, moaning. Suddenly rain fell. Big drops beat the izba window. Dark clouds rose up. Thunder rumbled. The popadyà covered her head with her mantle, moaning. 'Better the Lord should take us,' she said. 'Life, the beggar, will pass, bowing low.' The storm raged. The logs of the izba rocked. Darkness as of the Last Day looked in at the window. The lightning stabbed the eyes. The wind howled. The thunder split the ears. Lord, there never was known such a storm. Then it died suddenly. The pope looked out of the window and the popadyà threw off her mantle. 'Look! little father!' she said. She was standing behind the pope and looking out of the window towards the church. She crossed herself. 'Look at the ikon on the church wall!' she said. 'It shines! It is alight! The lightning has set it on fire.' She flew out of the door into the road with the pope waddling after her. Little fathers! it was a miracle! The blissful one was tired of being neglected. She sent the lightning from heaven and it struck the alms-box at the foot of the ikon and all the little silver coins flew out and formed a riza (the gold or silver cover of an ikon) on the blissful one. Choodo! choodo! (a miracle!) the pope and the popadyà cried out and ran to the belfry. They beat the tocsin on the church bells and all the villagers rushed out of their izbas and saw the wonder. Lord! what a time it was! People prayed on their knees before the wonder-working ikon all night. The blind and

The House in the Horseguards' Alley

the sick and lame came from all the villages around. Many were cured and left their crutches behind. Pilgrimages started. The Metropolitan came with the monks and held a moleben (Te Deum). Everyone gave money to the wonder-worker. Soon a great church was built and people came from all parts of Russia, from Tiphlis, from Siberia. In crowds they came."

"When did this happen?" I asked him.

"Just before the war," he replied. "If the gentleman wishes, I can take you there. It is not far from Petrograd."

I thanked him for the offer and preferred to see the wonder-working ikon when it was brought to the house for the benefit of mad Aunt Claudia. Stepan Piatko, it appeared, had induced the church authorities to have the ikon sent to the house. There would be a ceremony that evening in the drawing-room. I don't know what particular "miracle" Stepan Piatko expected the ikon to work on Aunt Claudia. I heard that she was deeply touched by this remarkable effort on his part to secure the help of heaven on her behalf. I put off going to the Ballet Russe that evening for the express purpose of seeing the wonderful ikon and what effect it would produce on the poor, mad woman. Perhaps she was not mad but weak-minded. At any rate, I met her in the corridor as she came upstairs to prepare the table for the ikon in the drawing-room. She was very agitated, nodding her head as though she had St. Vitus' dance, and muttering to herself.

"At last, there's a man who cares for me!" she kept repeating. "He does not spare himself for my sake."

Muttering and trembling, she passed down the corridor, a white lace kerchief thrown in a bride's fashion over her straggling, dishevelled, grey hair.

Chapter IX

THE HOUSE IN
THE HORSEGUARDS' ALLEY—*(continued)*

I

THERE HAD BEEN a heavy fall of snow just before dinner. It was about the end of November and still no settled wintry weather had set in. The snow had not yet succeeded in keeping its hold on the streets. Nevertheless, each fresh fall brought with it the hollow hush of the mantled roadways, deadening the sound of the traffic and offering a sort of invisible loud-speaker to the voices of the passers-by.

I waited in company with several members of the household in the overhanging window. The curtains had not been drawn so that we might peer out into the snow-lit dark and report the approach of the carriage bearing the wonderworking ikon. Madame Vadimsky was not at home. She had gone off with the Grand Duke S—— after an agitated evening, having played Chopin and sung Russian gypsy songs at the piano in her Rococo boudoir for the pacification of the Grand Duke during his closeted converse with her. She had sung with a depth of feeling and poetic rhythm that I had never associated with her usual, half-dazed look. One never knows what is in a person until something brings it out. What that was in her case, I had no chance of knowing at the time. All I knew was that she issued joyfully from her chamber, having altered her mind and decided not to stay for the reception of the wonder-working ikon. Instead, she ordered the car and left with her admirer, who, in order to avoid observation, always drove up in a common isvoschik.

Petrushka remained on his perch and amused himself by taking sly pulls at the women's hair. He wore his latest purple satin coat on which Madame Vadimsky had embroidered a strange coronet. It was unmistakably larger than any other she had sewn before, bravely done in gold thread and bearing obvious resemblance with the kind in use among members of the Imperial family. I could not help noticing from this trivial fact the direction which Madame Vadimsky's thoughts and dreams had taken. And why not? I knew already of Russian Grand Dukes who had defied Imperial convention and were living abroad, in London even, with the women they loved and had chosen to make their wives. I wished her good luck.

Count de Luze was not there. He had an appointment with certain officials of the Ministry of Justice, with whom he was using his influence to obtain some sort of preferential treatment for

The House in the Horseguards' Alley

the injured widow against the machinations of Peter Vadimsky.

Mad Aunt Claudia, for so she was always spoken of by the members of Madame Vadimsky's family, was downstairs in her flat preparing for the reception. She had spent more than an hour arranging a table at one end of the drawing-room, covering it with a white cloth, and decorating it with flowers (relics of the Grand Duke's offerings to his lady love) and dark, wax candles. A strange, ecstatic gleam had lit up her wandering eyes.

For the rest, the whole ceremonial seemed to be in the hands of its inspirer, Stepan Piatko. He had arrayed himself in a dress suit, with swallow tail coat and patent shoes. Chattering energy exuded from him without ceasing. Gone was the listless man whose life had revolved around eating and drinking, detective novels and the steaming baths. His endless talk was now accompanied by feverish action, edifying solicitude for the comfort of others, for the welfare of the offended and despised.

"Leave it to me. We will arrange everything!" were the two phrases that fell incessantly from his cherry-red lips. And everyone, startled out of his or her fleshly drowsiness by the contrast of Stepan Piatko's radiant energy and goodwill, resigned himself completely, murmuring to his neighbour: "What an energetic, kind-hearted fellow is Stepan Ivanich!"

Only Onofry, the manservant, accustomed to count for so much in the ordering of the house during the lifetime of his late bachelor master, went about with a frown and beat the air with his right hand, muttering : " The nameless one ! So he's found a burrow for himself ! " He had long been nursing a grudge against the new order of things.

II

We had been watching in the darkness for more than half an hour. Lights came and went, gliding pallidly over the bluish snow. Now and again a squad of soldiers, returning to the barracks of the Horse Guards near by, swung along the snow-muffled street with a plodding of heavy boots or singing a lilting song in unison. How their strong voices echoed down the quiet street and in the courtyard :

> "Bárinya, bárinya,
> V báraban oodárila
> Russ, dvah, tri . . . !"

Their mirth seemed to cleave a way through the shadows of the night. When they were gone, the snow-padded darkness fell back with a dead hush.

Tired of waiting, the young women fell to counting the number of passers-by, to guess one against the other whether the dim figure entering the top of the alley was a man or a woman and paying ten copecks for each false guess.

Mad Aunt Claudia sent up time after time to inquire if the " blissful one " was seen approaching. There were obviously great expectations in the flat below.

The girls, tired of guessing at men and women, turned to the lights of passing vehicles, motor or horse. They were looking up towards the avenue, when a sudden beating of horses' hoofs and a rumbling of wheels in the other direction drew their attention. A great, old-fashioned coach, drawn by three horses and swaying on heavy springs, turned the bend by Count Fredericks's house. The two women sprung up and rushed out into the hall, shouting " Eedoot ! eedoo-oot ! " (they come !).

In a moment the whole household was in a whirl of feverish excitement. Men and women rushed about, calling to one another " eedoot, eedoot ! " and knocking over chairs in their agitation. The servants all rushed in from the kitchens and pantries, blocking the doorways and crossing themselves.

Outside, I saw the great coach draw up at the archway. Stepan Piatko rushed out with a flaming wax taper and wrenched open the door. In the flickering light of the broad wick the round, bearded faces of three monks appeared. They stepped out, their shadows dancing black and ominous on the white snow. Crossing themselves, they turned to the open door of the coach and bowed low. Some flakes of falling snow flecked their black gowns and melted in their long hair. From the dark interior of the coach a fourth monk appeared, holding against his breast a shining ikon festooned with flowers and ribbons. Stepan Piatko bowed deeply, crossing himself without ceasing.

Suddenly from the archway the figure of a woman clad from head to foot in white rushed out and fell down before the wonder-working ikon. She threw back her head, looking up at it, then crossed herself and bowed down till her forehead touched the snow. Stepan Piatko had gone with the taper, showing the way. The white woman and the black monk seemed for a moment like two shadowy figures from an unreal world. They were gone an instant later into the house, the ikon being " rushed " from stopping-place to stopping-place.

The monks came up the carpeted stairway with mournful, long-drawn intonings in voices that seemed to ooze out from some deep, rumbling sepulchre. They droned lethargically, choosing the lowest possible pitch and waddling like great fat penguins. Their " Go-o-spo-o-di-i Po-o-mi-i-loo-oo-i-i " 's (Lord have mercy) sounding like the dull mooing of a company of cows.

A draft of sickening incense blew up with the cold wind from the open street door.

I stood at the top of the stairs watching the procession mount. Everybody in the house had gone down to welcome the " blissful one ". They crowded behind the ikon, crossing themselves and bowing. When the fat monk bearing the ikon passed into the drawing-room, I saw for the first time the woman in white. To my amazement, I recognized mad Aunt Claudia, dressed like a bride with white satin dress, white shoes and veil and carrying the curled white chrysanthemums which the Grand Duke S—— had offered that afternoon to Madame Vadimsky. . . .

III

The strangest thing happened at that visit of the wonder-working ikon. Whether it was part of Stepan Piatko's philanthropic schemes for the "offended and despised" or just a sudden whim of mad Aunt Claudia, it would be hard to decide. Anyhow, the mad woman's alarming conduct took the family by surprise and confirmed them in their belief that she was on the verge of dangerous insanity.

"This is final," one of them said to me in the hall, as the droning proceeded in the drawing-room before the ikon, placed on the white-robed table. "What further proof is necessary that she is stark mad? She should be put away. She may do serious harm next time."

Stepan Piatko, however, was not of this opinion. He quite agreed that Aunt Claudia was mad, but that it would be wrong to put her away for the sake of such harmless outbursts. She had lucid intervals. Besides, human feeling commanded us to shield and cherish her in her misfortune. Wasn't she a droll thing? She had actually taken it into her head that he was in love with her. Silly creature! He had only tried to make her feel that there was someone in the world who cared for her and tried to make her lonely life more bearable. But she had got the idea fixed in her head. She had actually dressed herself up like that because she believed she was going to be betrothed to him that evening after the ceremony with the ikon. No! it was useless to be angry with her or want to get rid of her. One had to humour her, let her believe she was getting what she imagined.

"Leave it to me!" he repeated. "We will arrange everything!"

He informed the household one after the other of his intentions. He would let the monks perform his betrothal with mad Aunt Claudia lest any hitch in her mad intentions should cause her to lose her head altogether and send her raving. She ought not to be thwarted. Lord have mercy! why, it might even be the saving of her! Wonders were always being worked. The ikon was there for that. Leave it to him. He would arrange everything.

So to him it was left. The mock betrothal took place and when the wonder-working ikon was taken away by the monks in the troika coach, mad Aunt Claudia, in her betrothal veil and dress, sat down at the piano and sang in a terrible voice: "The Song of the Volga Pirate".

Everybody applauded and encored the poor woman. It was a dismal song, hardly appropriate for the festive occasion, even though it was a mock one. For one thing, the bold pirate threw his beautiful bride overboard on the honeymoon night. I don't know whether Aunt Claudia glimpsed in her madness any prospect of similar treatment at the hands of her " betrothed ".

IV

Madame Vadimsky arrived home from her evening with the Grand Duke rather earlier that night than was her wont. She appeared about half-past eleven, while the household were still talking and sipping tea round the silent samovar. Thirsting for tea, she ordered the charcoal to be relighted. When this was done, she sat down at the table by the side of the hissing samovar and listened to the animated description of the night's events by the whole family. Stepan Piatko, as usual, managed to get the lead, subduing the weaker spirits into silence.

"Just leave everything to me," he declared. "All will be well. One must humour these patients. Perhaps it would be better if somehow we arranged to be married. Aunt Claudia wouldn't know that it was only a mock ceremony. It would fulfil all her deranged imagination. No possible harm could come of it. On the contrary, she would be well disposed and perhaps I might manage to bring her round to our side against that ne'er-do-well. It seems to me, at least, that a little deception of that sort would make everything work out all right. What then? Is it not a mad woman's whim ? "

The Blue Steppes

This he said, shrugging his shoulders and spreading out his flabby hands. Madame Vadimsky did not quite like the idea of trifling with the Church's ceremonies even to humour a mad woman.

" Leave it to me ! " he urged. " We will arrange everything."

Seemingly, matters were left to his handling. He always managed to have his way in the long run, finding resistance a mere matter of half a dozen words and a sigh. At that moment, however, something happened which switched off all discussion of the subject.

Poor Madame Vadimsky ! The fates seemed to have contrived a mortal conspiracy against her. When this new blow was struck, she looked so haggard and thunderstruck that one almost wanted to take her into one's arms to shield her from her own bewilderment. For all her stately beauty and moulded build, she seemed to fade away spiritually beneath the buffets of fate.

How she blanched when Onofry brought her the news ! The front door bell had rung and he had found outside a man with a portmanteau in his hand.

" He's waiting in the hall, your excellency," Onofry announced. " He says he's just arrived from Brazil and wants you to put him up. The hotels are full with the military."

" Brazil ? " she asked, staggered by the announcement. " What's his name ? "

" He wouldn't say, your excellency. He said you would understand. From Brazil."

The House in the Horseguards' Alley

She rose from the table, holding out both her beautiful hands before her and staring open-mouthed.

"It is he!" she stammered to the bewildered family.

"Who? who?" they clamoured, rising up noisily from their seats with that familiar panic which sweeps Russians so often.

"Klein!" she replied. "My first husband!"

"What does he want? tell him to go away!" Stepan Piatko growled heavily, making towards the hall door. "What daring is this, if you please?"

He went out into the hall, forgetting in his excitement to utter his familiar pacifying phrase: "Leave it to me!" though from the manner in which he took the matter into his hands it was evident he meant it.

We heard his voice, raised to a high, angry pitch, bombarding the unwelcome visitor: "You, brother, have come to the wrong place. Here are different arrangements from those you left. There is nothing for you to seek here. This is not a charity institution. . . ."

The other man's voice was equally loud and forceful.

"Who are you to talk to me in this manner? I am the father of my son, who is here in the house. I will be near my son. What does it matter if my wife is divorced from me? She is a widow now and I have divorced my second wife. Are *you* anxious to marry her? What are you doing in the house? . . ."

The Blue Steppes

While the altercation went on, Madame Vadimsky took her son of ten into her arms, sat down by the samovar again and threw out stammering scraps of enlightenment on the situation. She had lived with Klein five years. He was an official in the Foreign Office. She divorced him. They were miserably poor, while she had expensive tastes he could not afford to satisfy. He found another woman, and went to Brazil in the Russian service. She had never heard a word from him since, though he had sent a postcard to his son on his name's day each year. What could she do? How every hand seemed to be hard upon her!

The angry words in the hall were suddenly cut short by the appearance of a short, thick-set man of about thirty-five in the doorway of the dining-room. He threw a rapid glance at the astonished faces presented to him, and, catching sight of his young son in his former wife's arms, threw out his arms with a tremendous gesture of welcome and appeal, crying out in a loud, emotional voice: " Kotya! my darling son! Papa has come back!"

The boy hesitated for a moment, looked up into his mother's eyes, then, tearing himself away, rushed across the room and flung himself into the man's outspread arms. Kisses, huggings and " goo-goo " murmurings followed. Impossible for me to describe the orgy!

"Papa will sleep in my bed to-night. I will sleep on the ottoman," the boy declared, turning to his mother.

So it was arranged. M. Klein, smiling and

bowing, kissed his wife's hand and the hands of the rest of the women, shook hands with the men and took his seat at the table for refreshment from the samovar.

I left the dining-room about one in the morning, the descriptions of life in Brazil and the general outpouring of news to the traveller still showing no signs whatever of coming to an end.

The divorced husband seemed as happy and cosy as though the shadow of divorce had never entered his life, while Madame Vadimsky seemed to forget all her troubles in the anodyne of talk. Even Stepan Piatko seemed to have capitulated, drinking his endless glass of tea and chatting with the newcomer as though he were the most welcome of guests.

Chapter X

THE HOUSE IN
THE HORSEGUARDS' ALLEY—(*continued*)

I

M. KLEIN left early next morning before Count de Luze arrived. No doubt he had been given to understand, as Stepan Piatko afterwards boasted, that his presence in the house was undesirable. The threads of his and his ex-wife's lives had been torn too far asunder to be brought together again so easily. Moreover, her own loose ends were waiting to be linked up with those of one or other of the two aspiring noblemen. It had, however, been recognized that he had some sort of family claim over his son. But that was not sufficient to have him in the house. Stepan Piatko, therefore, with deep insight into the grave possibilities of the situation, took it upon himself to voice the widow's sentiments and succeeded in inducing the importunate man to retire to an hotel. Not, however, before the latter had claimed the use of one of the motor-cars. How the vigilant, forceful Stepan had yielded to this demand was not adequately explained by him. All we knew was that the ex-husband had

The House in the Horseguards' Alley

left about eight o'clock with the yellow car, saying that he needed it for his errands and would thus save his izvoschik fares. Anyhow, he brought the car back to the garage each night, mounted the stairs to visit his son, and thus found an opportunity to see his ex-wife whenever she was at home for the evening.

To put an end to this practice, Count de Luze came to the fore. He had been seriously alarmed by the unexpected advent of the ex-husband and taken to imbibing " phytin " with his meals. He suggested that the yellow car should be got rid of, or hired out. It would be a profitable business, making up a little for the financial loss caused by Peter Vadimsky's misbehaviour.

Seeing an advertisement in the *Novoye Vremya*, he begged me to call at the American Embassy. The American Ambassador was looking for a car to hire by the month. Count de Luze thought that, being English, I should be better able to explain the terms. The Ambassador received me himself and was most agreeable. The terms were soon settled, and with diplomatic dignity the Ambassador turned over a paperweight on which was written : " Time is money ". At this silent hint, I retired.

Thus the yellow car was disposed of for a while. When the ex-husband came for it and discovered it was gone, he accepted the situation with calm. Instead of going on his errands on foot, he entered the house and had tea with his son at the morning samovar, ending by going to this son's bedroom, which had a door communicating with Madame Vadimsky's bedroom, and holding a conversation with her through the key-hole.

Thus it came about that the ex-husband plied his suit in the morning at the bedroom door, Count de Luze followed with his about midday at the bathroom door, while the Grand Duke S—— took up the thread about five o'clock in the Rococo boudoir.

It was the ever vigilant Stepan Piatko that kept all three from clashing. He shuffled the ex-husband out of the house before twelve, manoeuvred Count de Luze back to his Red Cross work before five and kept the way clear for the Grand Duke S——.

Matters with Peter Vadimsky, however, were not going smooth. Count de Luze's efforts at the Ministry of Justice had so far met with little success, while the income from the offices of the *Petrograd Chronicle* was seriously diminished at the instigation of the ne'er-do-well Peter.

The alarming advent of Madame Vadimsky's ex-husband had put off for a while all discussion of the mock marriage of Stepan Piatko with mad Aunt Claudia. His wits were too well occupied with steering the new arrival out of the course of matrimony or any other form of aspiration to the widow's fortune.

Aunt Claudia, however, caused much amusement by going seriously about the business of

The House in the Horseguards' Alley

getting her trousseau together. She brought out sundry little hoards of gold from mysterious hiding-places and, escorted by Madame Vadimsky's widow sister, visited the shops on the Nevsky Prospect, choosing dainty, lace-trimmed underwear and luxurious corsets.

When she brought back the roll of Liberty satin she had bought at the English Magazine for her bridal robe, she called all the household down to her flat and unfolded the shimmering white stuff for their admiration. How often during that little visit she turned to the pierglass and trimmed the straggling grey locks of her hair, tucking them up beneath the spray of orange-blossom she had just bought! There were moments when her comment and genuine delight seemed quite normal, though she would always harp back to the fate of the bride of the Volga pirate, declaring that she was arraying her body for paradise.

The more attachment she displayed to the fixed idea of marrying Stepan Piatko, her " betrothed ", the deeper was the gloom and madness into which she plunged by way of re-action. At one moment she was ecstatic with thoughts of marriage, at another depressed with thoughts of death, threatening to drown herself. To prevent this, Stepan Piatko always hovered about her except when he was acting as a sort of master of ceremonies to the rival suitors.

He openly declared that if he could have a chance of searching mad Aunt Claudia's clothing he was sure he would find the picture of the Virgin of Kasan on the back of which the late M. Vadimsky was supposed to have written his will and on which Peter Vadimsky was staking his larger claim. Unfortunately for Stepan, Aunt Claudia never undressed without locking the door of her room. On the other hand, everyone feared to let her use the bathroom as she had already been rescued once from attempting to drown herself in the bath. She never ceased declaring that she had hidden the holy picture somewhere and would one day remember. Stepan left no stone unturned to hasten this happy event. His "betrothal" was one effort in that direction I am certain, his forthcoming "marriage" another.

In order to hurry up this desirable state of mind, Stepan now urged the "marriage" should take place at an early date. Aunt Claudia was delighted and insisted quite naturally in sending an invitation to her only relation, Peter Vadimsky, at his newly acquired house in Gatchina. Stepan tried his utmost to persuade her that he was a ne'er-do-well and would bring no honour to the ceremony. Mad as she was, Aunt Claudia stood her ground. She would not think of giving her hand in marriage unless it was done with the assistance of her only relation. She was not a common girl picked up in the gutter. She had relations who could testify to her honour and condition. Her nephew would have given her away from under his own roof if he had been alive.

As his son was living, the only male relation she had, she would not think of marrying without his presence. Such insistence on "principles" finally convinced Stepan, the emancipated intelligent, that Aunt Claudia was really out of her mind.

Whether Stepan sent the letter of invitation to Peter Vadimsky or whether Aunt Claudia posted it secretly during one of her shopping expeditions, I cannot say. When she was not off her head with ecstasy or off her head with gloom, she must have used some method in her madness. Peter Vadimsky got to know of the forthcoming "marriage", without doubt. His reaction took a startling turn. None of the household expected him to appear at the ceremony. Appear, however, he did, though a little sooner than they expected.

II

I was about to draw the curtains of my bedroom window overlooking the inner court, when the movements of certain dark figures under the carriage archway attracted my attention. It was late at night, about twelve o'clock, I think. I had been to a theatre and afterwards had tea with the household in the dining-room. I had left them there, only Madame Vadimsky being absent in town.

I should not have paid any further attention to the figures if I had not seen one of them creep stealthily into the yard and look up at the windows. He stood for a few moments gazing at the bright light in the dining-room, then tiptoed back to his companions with both arms swaying as though he were balancing himself on a tight-rope. There was a confabulation for a few moments and then one shadowy figure went to Aunt Claudia's door and held his arm out towards the lock.

Thinking there was mischief afoot, I rang the bell to summon Onofry. He came in a second, saw the men and went off like a shot to raise the alarm. He was certain they were burglars.

A few moments later, Stepan Piatko, Ivan, his brother, Madame Vadimsky's brother, the fiancé of her widowed sister, the chef and the yardman rushed from one of the back stairs across the yard and tackled the burglars. Instead of encountering resistance, they found the men quite calm and collected. They pointed to the open door and said something.

Stepan and his crew entered Aunt Claudia's flat, while the three men remained outside. There was calm for a while, till a pistol-shot rang out and two men ran out, one of whom was carrying mad Aunt Claudia in his arms. I expected to see Stepan Piatko follow with his company, but to my surprise the light from the open door was darkened by no man's form. I heard the throb of motor engines and the grinding noise of a car setting off.

Hurrying down to the scene of the affair, I

WOMEN MILITIA AT DRILL.

The House in the Horseguards' Alley

found the whole household in Aunt Claudia's hall, standing in a state of lingual panic around the prostrate form of Stepan Piatko. The fiancé doctor was bending over him and feeling his pulse. Stepan was panting woefully, his flabby face still less agreeable to look at and deathly pale. No wound, however, was found, neither did the minutest search for the mark of the bullet in the walls or ceiling reveal any trace of it.

The shot remained a mystery until Peter Vadimsky himself explained in the letter he sent next day that he had only fired a blank cartridge. He had decided to look after mad Aunt Claudia and prevent any " mocking " of his only relation by Stepan Piatko. He baldly declared that the latter wished to marry her because of her half-share in her nephew's estate according to the terms of the will on the back of the mislaid picture of the Virgin.

There was great consternation in the house, as can be well imagined. Nevertheless, during her absence, Aunt Claudia's flat was subjected to a thorough search for the missing picture. It was nowhere to be found. From that it was concluded that she must wear it somewhere about her person in one of the many pockets she was accustomed to have in her garments for the secretion of banknotes.

Stepan Piatko held a council of war with the male members of the household and decided that something must be done to get Aunt Claudia back, by kidnapping, if necessary, after the example of Peter Vadimsky. He brought out his revolvers and I fancy he did not resort to the delicacy of having them loaded with blank cartridges. In fact, he discussed that matter and came to the conclusion that wolf had been shouted once too often. Extensive plans were laid to find out when Peter Vadimsky was likely to be away from home, and to use that all-powerful weapon in Russia, the bribe. Stepan himself went down to Gatchina to sound the possibilities of bringing Peter's domestics into the plot. The ne'er-do-well had taken to himself a wife and established himself in an elaborate bourgeois manner.

Stepan Piatko's artful plans, however, were brought to nought by an unforeseen turn of events. Aunt Claudia herself returned to the house in the Horseguards' Alley the third day after her kidnapping. She had hailed the first izvoschik she saw passing the house after she had recovered from her prostration at being forcibly separated from her "betrothed". Peter Vadimsky was out of the house at the time, and not all the endearing charms of his young wife could succeed in convincing mad Aunt Claudia to stay.

Peter Vadimsky, however, on hearing of her departure, rang up his step-mother on the telephone and seemed to console himself for the loss of his aunt by declaring that he had revealed to her all the base intentions of Stepan Piatko and of the household in general. There would now be

The House in the Horseguards' Alley

little likelihood of her falling into the trap. Moreover, he called on Aunt Claudia with his young bride the same evening to thank her for coming to his house-warming.

Aunt Claudia, nevertheless, celebrated the occasion by stealing out of the house the same night and throwing herself into the Moika, one of the small canals near by. From this she was rescued by a sailor, taken to a hospital and brought home only after much telephoning on the part of Stepan to all the police-stations of the town. After that, everyone considered the mock marriage to be an absolute and immediate necessity. Humanitarian sentiments made the house ring with echoes. Pity, sad-eyed and gently shrugging its shoulders, stole hourly through rooms. "Of course!" it murmured, pouting its lips and inclining its head to one side, its palms outstretched and open. "It would be inhuman not to commiserate her."

So it was arranged that some sort of mock marriage ceremony should be performed in one of the monasteries of Petrograd. For a consideration many a celebrant would be forthcoming to perform this barren ritual "in the name of humanity", as Stepan Piatko was so fond of expressing it.

III

The days slipped by without any fresh development. I had a good deal of translating work to do and had borrowed a typing machine so that I could do everything in my room without bothering to walk across the frozen streets of the town or trying to hang on to the evil-smelling, crowded trams with the skin of my teeth. The lovers' rondo continued its tiresome refrain day after day, but still no final flourish was forthcoming to wind it up at last. Madame Vadimsky, I am sure, must have had the patience of Job.

Mad Aunt Claudia's "marriage" was put off indefinitely because no suitable monk and place had been found for the ceremony. After all, it was a mock performance and it was undesirable that people should talk about it. The alarmists would not understand that it was just a piece of well-doing "in the name of humanity". Stepan Piatko, however, had taken to cultivating a pious friendship with a dissolute monk at the great monastery of St. Alexander Nevsky. The disorderly scenes occurring at that institution were the common talk of the town. They outvied the awful things attributed by decadent society to Rasputin. Whether they corresponded to reality or were just the depraved fictions of a sordid hankering for scum which had taken hold of all classes and professions, I could not say. I only knew from one or two visits I had paid to the famous monastery that dissolute scenes were quite probable. The convent corridors had been crowded with fashionable women, mostly neurotic and hysterical, visiting some fashionable monk with a tale of marital woe. In fact, it was a common practice for them to go there both for consolation and to arrange their divorces with the Holy Synod.

The House in the Horseguards' Alley

Now and again a drunken monk staggered down the corridor, ogling the women and pawing them. The cleansing broom of the church was held back far too long, either by the intrigues of the political Synod or by the all-enduring indifference of the Russian character. I had no doubt, therefore, that Stepan Piatko would soon reap the reward of his friendship with the monk.

One night Aunt Claudia was called to array herself in her bridal dress. I did not see her personally, having been out at the time. When I arrived home about seven, I found the house deserted. Onofry was in the dining-room and informed me that dinner would be at a later hour. I looked at the table and saw that it was laid for a feast. Rows of wine glasses, bell-shaped, decreasing in size from the tall champagne glass to the tiny liqueur thimble, stood before each plate. Orchids raised their showy heads above silver flower-bowls, grouped about a large, white wedding-cake. It neither suggested that a tremendous war was in progress at the front nor hinted that the Imperial ukase forbidding the sale of alcoholic drink had stirred the English Press to peans of praise. It is only just and true to remark that I never came across a single family or person of means outside the Tsar's household who obeyed that ukase. The prohibition was practised only by those who had no means or opportunity for doing otherwise, in the same way that the Soviet caste later on indulged freely in the wine of the bourgeois cellars they monopolized while maintaining the prohibition for the common people.

I asked Onofry what the feast was for. He beat the air with his hand and uttered some sort of stifled curse.

" It is he ! " he said : " Stepan Ivanich. They have taken Claudia Grigorievna to be married. They say ' married '. Better they said ' buried '. Little she knows what she's about or what he's about either. But wait ! I swear by the godkin in the corner he will sit in the galosh ! " (in the soup !).

He turned to the ikon in the corner of the room and crossed himself.

" I have lived to old age, but not to such stupidity. Never were there such things in this house in master's time. Women ! Yes, three at a time. A merry one was the dead master. He sinned. But never this ! A mad old woman, and in the name of the Father, the Son and the Holy Ghost ! Never this abomination ! The dead one never married at law."

He muttered sullenly, shifting about the table and arranging the things.

Having arranged to go with a friend to see Tolstoy's *Fruits of Enlightenment*, I took a snack and went off into the snowy night. When I returned the feast was over. At least, as far as the " bride and bridegroom " were concerned. Russian marriages usually take place in the evening and the happy couple retire to their room soon after their health has been drunk.

The House in the Horseguards' Alley

In this case they had retired to Aunt Claudia's flat downstairs.

Next morning I went into the dining-room for breakfast about eight o'clock and was surprised to find the entire household out of bed. They were talking wildly and gesticulating. From their happy faces I gathered that something very agreeable had entered their lives. Madame Vadimsky was there in her kimono, nursing Petrushka and kissing him occasionally as though she could not help venting her happiness on some fondling or other. My advent was greeted by a general shout of " Nashli ! " (found !).

" What's found ? " I asked, wondering at all the excitement.

" The picture of the Kazan Virgin," they replied.

Stepan Piatko, I saw, was the hero of the hour. Bottles of champagne stood on the table and glasses were constantly filled.

I sat down and heard the story from Stepan Piatko himself. He seemed infinitely pleased with himself.

" It was the only way to get hold of it," he said, showing me the little oblong card with the picture of the Virgin. " I guessed she must have had it somewhere about her person because she never would let anyone come near her when she undressed at night. The ' marriage ' went off all right. During the night I gathered up her clothes and searched them. The picture was actually sewn up in the lining of her body-warmer.

But it's no good as evidence. Look at it. It is all torn and splashed with ink. No one can make out what it means."

I looked at the card and saw that the handwriting had been scratched and obliterated. Whether Stepan Piatko had taken that precaution, it was hard to say. It was so filthy, one hated to touch it even. Anyhow, Stepan Piatko didn't destroy it now that it was in his possession, but smilingly declared that it would be faithfully preserved in order to prove that Aunt Claudia's picture of the Virgin had no more chance of being accepted as the will and last testament of the late M. Vadimsky than any other scrap of paper scribbled with hieroglyphics.

The card was duly handed over to Madame Vadimsky's lawyers and the ne'er-do-well Peter immediately informed of the collapse of his case.

IV

Madame Vadimsky went about with a radiant smile that morning. But not for long. She had arranged for a gypsy fortune-teller to call and tell her something about her future. I fancy she was very anxious to bring the Grand Duke S—— to some sort of declaration of his intentions.

The dark, hideous old gypsy, smelling rankly of camp fire, told her that she must beware of a fair enemy. This gave her much cause for agitated thinking. She could think of no fair enemy she knew. The problem, however, soon solved itself.

About half-past two the same afternoon, a sumptuous motor-car drew up at the front door. I was just going out at the time and caught sight of a very pink, scintillating beauty, wrapped in ermine, sitting inside the car. A grave young footman got out from the front to open the door for her. I saw her pass over the snowy pavement, buoyant, fluffy, and light as an Easter chicken. She seemed to irradiate the charm of feminine softness. I still remember vividly the flash of her eyes and teeth as she smilingly alighted. . . .

When I returned for tea, I was informed that Madame Vadimsky was seriously ill and had taken to her bed. There had been a terrible scene in the Rococo boudoir. From one or the other of the family I gathered that the strange, fair visitor was no other than the actress, Madame Tinska, who lived in a beautiful palace on the banks of the Neva near the Winter Palace. Whatever had she come to seek for at the house in the Horseguards' Alley? A simple affair! The doctor fiancé of Madame Vadimsky's widowed sister told me all about it.

Madame Tinska had arrived for the purpose of explanations. She had heard that the Grand Duke S—— had been carrying on an intrigue with Madame Vadimsky and had come with an iron determination to put things right. She could not allow the Grand Duke to open up new avenues of adventure while she was his mistress. She would be sole possessor of his affections or not at all. Madame Vadimsky had felt greatly offended. She had revolted against the insinuation that the Grand Duke S—— treated or intended to treat her as his mistress. Her own, and she trusted his, intentions had been honest all along. Then Madame Tinska had laughed at the idea that the Grand Duke could possibly have " honest " bourgeois intentions. It was forbidden by the State! There had been a scene. Tempers had risen and voices had been raised. The climax was reached when Madame Tinska, goaded on by jealousy, seized a signed photograph of her Grand-ducal lover, which she happened to catch sight of on the writing table, and tore it into shreds. After that, the jealous mistress fled from the house, beside herself. . . .

The ringing of the front door bell announced the arrival of the Grand Duke himself for his afternoon visit. When he was shut in with Madame Vadimsky, who for the purpose of receiving him had left her bed for the divan in the Rococo boudoir, there began a great exercise in tiptoeing on the part of the household. They walked about in breathless silence, almost as though they feared to hear themselves breathe. Their agitated state of mind evidently hindered them from sitting down. Moreover, the anxiety of Stepan Piatko constantly led him down the corridor in the direction of the boudoir door, where he would remain mysteriously silent, returning at intervals on tiptoe to the dining-room and making nervous signs of irritation to those who ventured to ask in bated breath what turn the interview had taken.

I went about my business long before the household recovered their voices and soles.

Like the passage of a great ocean liner bound for a far goal, the Grand Duke's visit left behind a foaming pathway in the cloven waters of Madame Vadimsky and her household's spirit. The blow struck by the irate mistress was soon followed by that of the Grand Duke. He could offer no more than "love", pure and simple, without any reference to ceremonies outside his Imperial caste.

Poor Madame Vadimsky, always so kind and gentle, stood this last blow bravely. The visit of the irate mistress had prostrated her. That of the Grand Duke, however, more distressing in its consequences, seemed to fill her with bracing resolution. Perhaps it had settled at last the haunting doubts and indecisions that had cast such an enervating shadow over her spirit. She must have felt free, for the next day she signified her intention to Count de Luze of accepting his proposal to become his wife.

As for the ex-husband, who threatened to make himself a nuisance, he was removed by the stroke of his own hand. He arrived as usual the morning after the Grand Duke S——'s fatal visit and was told the nature of the latter's proposal. Indignation rose in the man like a storming passion. He would not allow his "wife" to be insulted! He would give his last drop of blood to wipe out the insult! She was the mother of his son!

So great was his anger that Madame Vadimsky feared to tell him of her decision to become Countess de Luze. She trembled to think what the infuriated ex-husband would do. He implored her to re-marry him, but she gently declined and shut herself up in her boudoir. Lashed to fury, the man waited about the yard until the Grand Duke arrived to pay his court and renew his persuasions. When he arrived, the ex-husband sprang out from behind a stack of logs and struck him a blow on the cheek.

"That's for your insult to my wife!" he cried out. "I challenge you to a duel!"

Duelling was a common occurrence among husbands and lovers. It will be remembered that the elder brother of Prince Felix Yousoupoff was shot dead in such a duel just before the war. In this case, however, the Grand Duke S—— simply had the ex-husband arrested and sent to the army in the Caucasus.

Going into the house after this little affray, he was met by Stepan Piatko, who coldly informed him that Madame Vadimsky had decided to become the Countess de Luze, leaving him standing.

And so she did a few days later, budding out into one of the sweetest, kindest and most appre-

The House in the Horseguards' Alley

ciative patronesses of rising talent that ever graced Society.

Peter Vadimsky no longer entertaining designs on the flat I had been asked to occupy and my affairs calling me elsewhere, I left the house in the Horseguards' Alley, taking with me this unwithering bunch of memories.

Chapter XI

A GARDEN OF EDEN

WHEN THE GREAT TIDE of liberty and eloquence was surging about the foundations of the State and Kerensky was feeding the nation with stars, I took a trip to the Crimea. It was in June 1917. Seeing the chaos into which the country was sinking through the prating idealism and pathetic humanitarianism of the Socialists, I made every possible effort to get away to England. The dislocation of the ways of communication, however, prevented me from getting beyond the Finnish frontier. The British Consul in Petrograd told me that if I cared to wait long enough I might get a berth on a ship from Archangel, but for the time being everything was reserved for military and diplomatic persons.

"Take a holiday in the Crimea," he said. "I will let you know by telegram when there's a chance of getting a ship."

Accordingly, I gathered up my goods and left for the south. I had a young Moscow friend, who was staying with his uncle at a villa near

A Garden of Eden

Yalta, so I felt happy at the prospect of finding friends.

The train journey of a thousand miles was slow and tedious. Congestion reigned on the railways as everywhere else. For hours at a stretch it was impossible to get out of one's coupé without a struggle, warring with sheep-skinned peasants, exuding soldiers, and the usual garrulous army of chinovnicks on their annual trek to the country or the sea.

Indescribable were the scenes of disorder and confusion. As usual in Russia, everyone had brought the greatest possible amount of cumbersome luggage into the coupés and corridors.

Before the war, during my travels in Germany, the natives would always refer to confusion and disorder as " Polish management ", in Poland they would call it " Russian management ", and going further East, I found the Russians called it " Chinese management ". I suppose the Chinese have also some favourite way of fastening their contempt on the shoulders of their Eastern neighbours.

Here, at least, was a sight for the nether gods. A schoolmaster with his wife and three children had brought into the coupé five large pillows and blankets, two teapots and a kettle, various hampers containing cooking utensils and crockery, bed linen and clothes, boots and shoes tied together like onions, overcoats, large and small, tied round with a rope, and what annoyed one more than all, a family bath ! The wretched thing was rolled in and held in position between the opposite seats by one of the boys, a " gymnasist " in a black uniform and peaked casquet, who beguiled the time by beating out a melancholy tattoo on the tin bottom almost the whole of the journey.

"Why do you want to take a bath with you when you are going to the sea?" I asked, somewhere in the middle of the endless plain.

"That's for my wife," he said. "You see, she is 'grosse' and of course it wouldn't do for her to bathe in the open. We can carry the water up to the cottage."

"But couldn't you hire a bath down there," I asked. "There must be lots of baths for hire, besides private establishments."

He gave a contemptuous toss with his thin, bald head.

"What! Pay for someone else's bath, when I have my own! What nonsense!"

Unfortunately, it was the general sentiment outside the aristocracy. Only those who have seen the inside of a Russian railway station can realize what it led to. To make matters worse there was no forwarding company like Carter Paterson, and when the Americans attempted to set up an express delivery company in Russia, they were for some unknown reason debarred by the Government.

At Kharkov a woman got in with a coffin covered with silver paint, put the lid on top of the bundles on the rack and stood with the gruesome object outside in the congested corridor.

PARADE OF BOLSHEVIST WOMEN SOLDIERS.

[To face p. 168.

A Garden of Eden

When the conductor squeezed his way along, picking up tips here and there in accordance with the well-known maxim of the Russian railways: "no protest, no tip", he blinked at the woman with the coffin.

"What's this, if you please?" he asked in a voice of pretended surprise.

"An evident matter!" the woman replied, tugging at her black kerchief and fastening it tight under her red chin. "Even a hen wouldn't have to look twice to see whether it was a popcorn."

Sitting in my coupé, I couldn't help laughing in secret. These lashing answers were the speciality of the country in all classes. In educated and aristocratic circles, they rather shocked, but coming from hags and merry market-wives they had a racy flavour of the soil.

"This—er——" the conductor stuttered. "This must be taken out of the way. It is against the rules of the company."

"Indeed!" rejoined the woman. "There is nothing for you to oppress the people for. Not for you is the coffin, brother, though one day you will want one yourself. Why do you oppress the people? Yourself, you ride all day long and then you are not content. The others you persecute, though they would only ride as far as the little finger. Unconscionable! Where is your conscience, persecutor?"

The babbling woman went on without stopping, till the conductor beat the air with his hand as a sign of hopelessness and passed on.

At Sinelnikov a company of women soldiers of the Death Battalion were waiting at the station. They were a very inspiring sight, except for their broad breeches and high-heeled shoes. But they carried themselves manfully, shouldering their rifles and marching up and down the sandy platform with parade-day trimness. The sergeant-majoress was an obese lady with rather portly bearing, but she made up for this defect with a most invidious eye, a tossed-back, close-cropped head and a booming voice.

"Naza-a-ahd!" she shouted to the marching soldieresses (*soldatki*), thrusting out a chin, which I'm afraid was rather telescopic.

The soldieresses swung round with great precision and smartness, though one couldn't help noticing that it was not their rifles that got in the way but their hips.

Standing along the platform watching these operations were groups of peasant women. They made no scruple of venting their views.

"Daughters of Hades!" I heard one baba call out, spitting on the ground. "They couldn't wait till their husbands came home. They go, the shameless ones, to make love to the Germans. 'Tis man's job to fight, baba's to love."

"They go in order to fall prisoners to the Germans," another woman cried out, falling on to her sack of potatoes by way of illustration.

The chorus of disapproval was taken up violently all along the line, by the men especially. Yet it was because of the failure of the men and the breakdown of the patriotic spirit that these brave women had undertaken to set an example of fearlessness. They were going down to the July offensive of the Russian Army in Galicia which the Kerensky Government had at last found tardy courage to allow.

At Simpheropol I left the train and spent the night at an hotel, where for the first time it was announced that the Professional Union of Waiters had decided to forbid the acceptance of tips. Perhaps that accounted for the unusual size of the bill, for they charged me thirty shillings for a small bedroom in a stucco hotel, with no sheets to the bed! Travellers were expected to have their own.

Simpheropol lies at the foot of the Crimean hills. From there one was obliged to hire a motor-car or buy a place in the diligence. It had been the intention of the Tsars to keep the Crimea free from all innovations that would spoil its charms. Accordingly no railways were allowed to be constructed except to Sebastopol at one end of the peninsula and to Theodosia at the other. Jews also had been forbidden to enter this little garden of Eden, but with the downfall of Tsardom they were flocking in from all directions.

"How much did you pay for your pince-nez?" one of them asked as I took my seat in one of the motor-cars that plied between Simpheropol and Yalta.

"The Germans will win this war," he went on afterwards, carrying on that intense pro-German propaganda which was the work of the Russian Jews during the war. In this, however, they were seconded by many Poles, and by the Tartars, Finns and other nationalities in Russia. It seemed as though the poor Russians themselves had lost their voice, their head, their nationality and their country. After a drive of about forty miles through olive groves and vineyards, we came in sight of the sea, having mounted gradually to the top of a high plateau. There were thick woods here and it was cool and refreshing to drive along in the leafy shade after the hot stretches of dusty, boulder-bounded roads. During the journey I saw a strange sight. The ruts in the road went on in regular lines for miles and in one of them I saw what seemed to be a gigantic white post walking along the road. As we came nearer in the motor-car, we saw that it was moving along very swiftly. At night it would have looked just like a fantastic ghost. We saw at last that it was a column of white dust about twenty feet high and two feet broad twirling round and round with incredible swiftness and rushing along in the groove of a cart rut. We drove alongside this extraordinary phenomenon for miles and it was still rushing forward when we lost it from sight. The strangest part of all was that there was hardly any breeze at all.

We passed through many a Tartar village, saw slippered Mohammedans and women in airy trouser-bags, and topping the brow of the hill descended to the sea-board at Gurzuf. Then began a pleasant journey along the coast through

NOVO-SEMEIS.

sandy roads, past pleasant villas set in the midst of roses, magnolias, cypresses and odorous shrubs, till we came to Yalta, nestling with its golden-domed churches and white houses at the foot of a superbly upright sweep of wooded hills.

From here I was rushed on to Novo-Semeis, a small resort that lay in a secluded bend of the coast. The sky was intensely blue, the rays of the blinding sun beating down on the white road, the white villas and white-clothed people, till everything seemed like a long white blur. Only the tall cypresses, now rising up dark against the hilly background, now standing with inviting coolness against the shimmering mirror of the sea, splashed the scene with a relieving black. The air was full of the scent of roses and flowering shrubs, heavy with the burning breath of the sun and the exudations of the scorched trees, the slight salty tang of the sea. Sunburnt Tartars galloped by on their thick-set horses, their red tassels bobbing in the breezeless air, their white teeth gleaming, their dark eyes afire. Handsome women, clad in light dresses, showing an abundance of sunburnt skin, galloped at the sides of the Tartars, laughing and chattering.

I drove up to the Villa Sidorski and was effusively welcomed by my friend and his relations. The villa stood just on the edge of a cliff and caught the sunlight even when the rest of the place was wrapt in the shadow of the overhanging hills. There was a balcony attached to the room assigned to me. Stepping out on to it in order to

The Blue Steppes

view the sea and village, I was agreeably surprised to see the national Russian flag flying from several house-tops. It was the first time I had seen the old flag since the February revolution. I must confess it was a great relief to get away from the ubiquitous red flag, which was already beginning to stink in the nostrils of all decent beings. I was told that a patriotic society was holding a sports meeting for some charity purpose, so, wishing to add to the glory of the show, I took out my silk Union Jack and tied it on to the pillar of the balcony. Some time later a couple of frowsy individuals calling themselves the president and delegate of the local Soviet came to know what enemy flag it was. When told it was British, they declared it should be taken down, as Britain was a bourgeois, reactionary country and the cause of the economic breakdown in Russia by insisting on carrying on the war to a victorious end.

"We are all brothers now," the president declared. "We've no need to fight the Germans. We must fight Capitalism now."

Fight Capitalism! With the Germans at the door and a famine already creeping over the plains of Russia owing to disorganization. Yet here was this great mind ready to open the gates to the enemy and complete the wreck of organized society. Perhaps he has now grown up in wisdom, having seen his unhappy country lose more th n twenty millions of people by famine and slaughter. Brotherhood and the destruction of Capitalism! What a mockery the words seem after one has seen the picture. But at that time everything was hinged on visions and propaganda, poured out day after day in the Socialist and Communist Press. No doubt he had just been devouring Lenin's newspaper. Anyhow, I told him that my flag would remain there until he came to take it down himself, but having no crowd to support him in those parts, he withdrew with his companion.

Near the Villa Sidorski was a large establishment called Dolnikoff, a sort of hotel with spacious grounds. In the evening, when the sun had gone down behind the hills, people would flock into the large drawing-room to be amused by the celebrities who were staying there. Shaliapine would come along to sing. He lived along the coast and had just succeeded in killing a burglar who climbed into his bedroom. This event must have had an agitating effect upon his temper, for he flooded the drawing-room and the rose-covered terrace with such terrific rolls of sound that it was a relief to hide in the cavern under the sea-wall and listen to him from that seclusion. Floating rhythmically through the scented atmosphere, his songs would then seem like a Cyclopean singing heard in a dream. And when the moon rose resplendent over the waters, spinning a long, golden carpet down to one's very feet, it seemed as though one stood at the entrance to a palace of enchantment.

Another celebrity was Rachmaninoff. Unfortunately, all the aspirants to musical fame in the neighbourhood used to crash out his " Prelude " on their pianos into the grand morning air with such persistence that the unfortunate composer could never be induced to play it. His only wish was to forget that he had ever composed a line.

Drozdoff, the pianist, however, used to give excellent performances and did not refuse even to play the piano while the various young ballet dancers showed off their talents before their admiring mammas and friends and the general public. Whenever one went to the drawing-room one was certain to hear the tap-tap-tap of some pretty girl of ten or twelve practising Pavlova's " Swan's Death " on the tips of her toes and flapping her sinuous arms with mournful solemnity, while a poor down-trodden governess picked out Saint Saëns " Chant de Cigne " on the piano.

Madame Germanova, a celebrated Russian actress of the classic school, would entertain us with renderings of poetry. The tragic Muse was always heavy on her breast and she excelled in making one feel quite miserable. But she did it with such consummate art that one felt grateful to her.

Boating, bathing, tennis, and excursions on Tartar horses filled the daytime. There were ancient monasteries and relics of Genoese and Venetian civilization to be visited.

As for the people, their manners were as interesting as their morals. Of the younger generation hardly one couple had the husband or wife they arrived with. The elder people seemed still to retain a certain respect for the conventions, though evincing a perfect indifference to the actions of the younger people.

Madame Olga Novikoff once said of herself: "I am a nihilist so far as conventionalities are concerned,"[1] and in that, she voiced the basic sentiment of the nation. She also wrote: "There was in Russia a great tendency towards childishly extreme views. . . . Agnosticism and Positivism seemed more in accordance with 'the latest dictum of science', as they used to term it. Katkoff, the political writer, saw at a glance that such Radicalism could only bring his country to the verge of ruin. He seemed to foresee the nihilistic movement which came later, not in Russia only, but in the whole world, and it grieved and frightened him, because he knew his country well. Reckless, self-sacrificing Russians never stop half-way. You often see people, both in England and Germany, without any religious or moral belief; but they are kept in good order, and are harmless in their intercourse with others, simply because they are checked by all sorts of imaginary powers—be it Mrs. Grundy, be it the craving for respectability, or the prejudices of the upper ten. We Russians never kneel to deities of that kind. We must have something solid, a religious 'categorical imperative', as the Germans say."

This latter, however, as most of us recognize, took the form of the knout in Russia for many years. As for religious imperatives, they had disappeared entirely among the intelligentsia since the writing of that article in 1887 (December 17th and 21st, *Pall Mall Gazette*). All had been swept

[1] *The M.P. for Russia*, vol. i. p. 4.

away as " prejudice " and " relics of superstition ". Here, in the Crimea, the result of this decay was thrust upon one on all sides. The sea, the sands, the rocks, cypresses, heavy-scented shrubs and rose-twined walks were as a garden of Eden where the Fallen State seemed to run amok.

I will not describe these things, for fire and brimstone have fallen upon Russia, while the Bolshevists have made this hideous amorality and anti-conventionality the basis of their system. They have abolished " bourgeois " morality and prejudices, but the intelligentsia had abolished them in practice long before.

In the Crimea the wave of sex-communism and contempt for the conventions reached its most revolting height.

One could hardly believe that these were educated people, members of the aristocracy, the bureaucracy, the professions. Whom the gods will destroy, they first deprive of reason, has been only too true of unhappy Russia.

The " love " idea prevailing among the Russian intelligentsia is well illustrated in a poem by Igor Sievieryanin, a popular poet. His heroine declares :

"I'm in love with Love, though not believing in it.
I seek for Him, not knowing Him.
He doesn't exist, and yet He is in every man.
A lover goes away—it is no loss :
Already another comes along.
After laughter, sadness. After sadness, laughter.
Pretence alone is sin. Sin itself is sinless.
Convention ?—'Tis nothing but a halter
For a she-ass. But freedom is always a joy."

I might have felt somewhat terrified in this ghastly garden of Eden, but the greatest shock of all was when one of the best known British consuls arrived, having deserted his Russian wife and taken up with the wife of a Russian General. He was a man with a grown up family and bordering on sixty. I felt thoroughly ashamed of him. But my sentiments were to receive a yet harder blow, for when the Bolshevists got into power and they arrested one night the British representatives (Sir George Buchanan had left long before), they announced in *Izvietiya* that they found this British establishment overrun with orgiastic revellers.

The atmosphere of Russia seemed to infect all comers.

Charming princesses would come to the Crimea in order to have love intrigues with the handsome Tartar men, who usually escorted them on their galloping white horses to the hills and valleys about the coast. These men were tall and sunburnt, strongly built and with well-cut features, white, perfect teeth and fiery eyes. The charming Russian women admired them without stinting. Their greatest praise was summed up in the phrase one heard on all sides : " African blood ".

At the Villa Sidorski there came to stay a Russian sailor. He was serving on one of the battleships cruising about the Black Sea and had obtained a few days' leave. He was a man of about forty, handsome and black-bearded. Although he had enlisted as a plain sailor in the Russian Navy, he

The Blue Steppes

was a man of great wealth. His son and mistress were staying at the villa. The son was about eighteen, while the mistress had been his mother's sewing-maid. The mother had gone off with some other woman's husband, as was the great fashion, and the father had gone off with the maid. The revolution came and the father entered the Navy for some obscure reason. Now the maid was installed *mensa et thoro*, though without benefit of clergy, but in all things taken into the world as an equal. What did the world say? Nothing! What could it say when everyone was doing the same?

After a stay of about ten days, Andrey Lvoff, the sailor-millionaire, went back to his ship at Yalta and his eighteen-year-old son, a tall, hefty fellow with horse-like jaws and bones, made love to his father's mistress.

Marya Ivanovna was her name. She had fair hair and beady eyes, laughed after every word she uttered and snuffled her nose like a rabbit! She knocked at my door one evening and walked in boldly, her white heels tapping on the polished pine floor. There was a terrific thunderstorm going on outside. The lightning flamed blue and purple over the shrouded hills, the thunder cracked and boomed all around with Vulcanic fury. It was dark on the wind-lashed water, the clouds swelling earthwards like heavy black sails.

"Let me come and talk to you," she said, coming towards the window of the balcony where I stood watching the storm. "Jhootko!" (it's ghastly).

She pointed to the raging storm and sat down on the edge of the bed.

"Here's a deck chair," I said, bringing one in from the balcony.

She threw herself into the chair as though she no longer had the power to hold herself up.

"This awful storm," she went on in a voice that squeaked from the top of her throat. All her former exuberance of laughter had deserted her. "He's out there on the ship, Andrey Fomich Lvoff, I mean, my husband."

She turned her wedding-ring round on her finger contemplatively, though it was common knowledge they had never been married at law. But what of that? Freedom was the new gospel.

"A sailor's life," I replied, watching the sea. "A few ups and downs are to be expected. It will go by."

"All the same, it's ghastly," she rejoined mournfully. "It lies heavy on the soul. And there's Vassili (the eighteen-year-old son of her 'husband'). He pesters me all the time. Dersky takoi! (audacious one). I slapped his face, but still he pesters, more than ever. I said to him: 'How are you not ashamed? insolent cub!' But he: 'Is that how you talk to Andrey Fomich, baba?' And he pesters me still more audaciously. One wants to weep almost. 'How are you not ashamed?' I said. 'What would your father say?' And he, audacious one: 'Did he say anything when he left my mother for you?' I was angry. The insult was such. 'And your mother,' I said. 'Hasn't she gone with another? Am I not the same as she? What is to be said? We are lovers.' He glared. Jhootko! Such eyes and such strength! He seized me by the arm. It hurt. 'And now, we shall be lovers too!' he said. I cried for pain and slapped his face. Akh! What violence is in the world!"

She covered her face with her hands and sighed. Then she got up and went to the balcony to breathe the fresh air.

"Look ye," she said, resting her arm against the closed half of the French windows. "I want to talk to you. From the warm soul. You seem to me sympathetic, a decent one. Not like us Russians, always turning things inside out. Tell me. What do you think? How can I arrange myself? With Andrey Fomich, I mean. I love him. He loves me, painfully loves me. But he does not marry me. 'That,' he said, 'is past game. Superstition. Prejudice. Now there is free love. The rest is all dust-covered, out of date.' How can I arrange myself? I implored him. He would not hear. But I. . . . They say I am old-fashioned. New fashions are new fashions, but somehow, I like the old. Look now! I wanted to wear a ring. He gave me one. 'But in church,' I said. 'In the old-fashioned way.' 'Nobody marries now like that,' he said. 'Now is free love. Thou lovest, thou livest. The matter is finished.' And so, he would not. But I kept the ring. Now what do you think? Artful am I. I have a child. It is three months gone. I have not told him. But I must. I am full of hope. I will make him marry me in the old-fashioned way, before the priest or the law. Do you think he will be angry? Leave me? . . ."

The storm raged on and the woman's palpitating battle of hope and fear continued unabated. What could I do? I just listened, listened, waiting for the time when she would grow tired and seek other ears.

Somehow I realized that her aspirations were the last flickering glimmer of the old Christian soul of Russia, fast dying under the burning blasts of the "emancipated" Communistic age. Before the Bolshevists seized power, the intelligentsia had reduced the bonds of marriage to an absurdity in actual life. The Bolshevists reduced them to an absurdity at law, in the same way as they decreed the abolition of money by inflating the rouble to the point of worthlessness.

When I returned to Moscow from this garden of Eden, Lenin was already establishing this emancipated world with bombs.

Chapter XII

THE HOMES OF THE MIGHTY (PETROGRAD)

COUNT CLÉMÉTIEFF. Whisper the name to a Russian and he will understand more than if you had read him a chapter of Russian history. In fact, Count Clémétieff's illustrious ancestor was a great general in Peter the Great's adventurous campaigns. When one entered his palace on the French Quay in Petrograd, one stood near to the acme of European refinement and culture. Footmen, tall and stately, waited at the lofty entrance and were as mellow in manner as any Great Britain could boast. Apollos and Venuses gleamed white from their elevated positions and Renaissance beauties offered their rosy exuberances and grapes from the high, tapestried walls. Nor in this heaven of fine art were lacking the best works of modern Russian painters and sculptors, though nothing gross and Epsteinesque was allowed to mar the flight of the admiring eye towards the eternal beauty of the human mind in its efforts to express the ideal. The products of

The Homes of the Mighty (Petrograd)

the fine art of ugliness were left to be acquired by unrefined profiteers and exuberant Asiatics, or to repose in museums of curiosities. As Count Clémétieff himself explained when I congratulated him on his exquisite taste: " I will have nothing in my house that I cannot feel I could live with eternally. We become like the things we admire. Mere antiquities and modern 'Grausamkeiten', I leave to the museums of curiosities." And naturally, after such a lofty speech, I wondered what his wife was like.

In the vast library reaching to the roof of the palace, rare books and literary treasures were stored, while a brass engraving attached to the wall commemorated the various visits to the library by emperors and kings.

A beautiful private chapel was situated on the top floor and mellow-toned bells rang for vespers or mass from a turret. In the reading-room all the best English journals lay in rows on the table, and the only soap recognized in this very selective establishment was Pears.

When I saw Countess Clémétieff for the first time, I found her in perfect keeping with the spirit of the house. Fair, handsome and quiet-mannered, though with an abundance of wit and restful self-control, she had a peaceful English atmosphere of which she was very proud. Her family had been brought up by English governesses for generations. A thorough knowledge of languages was considered obligatory on all members of the upper classes and for this purpose children were given into the hands of English and French governesses almost from birth. In this way the upper classes spoke foreign languages with wonderful ease and correctness, whereas the ordinary Russian, left to the desultory instruction of the schools, showed no more aptitude for foreign languages than a Frenchman.

The preferences of the Court lay towards the English tongue for intimate use and Countess Clémétieff showed the same leaning in educating her children. She had, however, employed, when they were young, a Frenchwoman, who had afterwards married an Armenian, repented very soon of this step, and fled for protection to her generous ex-employer with endless lamentations on the Oriental baseness of the Armenian male. She had been received back into the house with open arms and had assumed the rôle of indispensable guardian of the destinies of the entire household. Unlike so many highly cultivated French people one met with in Russia, she showed an extraordinary animosity towards everything English. Once, at a tea party at which the Grand Duchesses Olga and Tatiyana were present, she resented the praise bestowed by the latter on a little English girl of five or so, the daughter, I gathered, of Mr. Lindley, of the British Embassy.

"What a pretty child," the Grand Duchess exclaimed aside to some grown-ups. "I always admire the beauty of English children."

Madame Adjhemian, as the Frenchwoman was called, rolled her dark eyes and exclaimed:

The Homes of the Mighty (Petrograd)

" Mais, Altesse, la beauté Française, c'est la beauté céleste ! "

" Iln'y a pas de doute ! " the Grand Duchess replied. " And all little children come from heaven."

Madame Adjhemian's great delight was to get Russian members of the diplomatic service to relate their experiences of England. She had a sharp, ready, malicious tongue, which many Russians, who are adepts in a certain bitter, iconoclastic cynicism, found much to their taste. On Sundays especially, or at any of the great luncheon parties given by Count and Countess Clémétieff on feast days, she used to set the ball of cynicism rolling. I remember on one occasion a certain Prince Drouki, who was attached to some diplomatic or military mission in London, holding forth to his end of the luncheon table on the comical codes of the British. He must have been unaware either that I knew Russian or that I was quite capable of hearing his outpourings while carrying on a conversation with my neighbour. Russians, it should be borne in mind, never consider themselves under any obligation whatever towards a person with whom they have had an intrigue not exactly within the scope of legality. When they have finished with that person they will cry her name from the housetops and enlarge in a mixed public on all the intricacies of their experiences.

" Puritanism," Prince Drouki held forth, " is never dead in England. About six months before I left I went to stay at a country house with

The Blue Steppes

Mrs. Z——, a remarkably fine woman with the figure of a first-class filly. Her head was fair, something like a Bianca Capelli, and she held it up in a fashion a little too *voulu*. Her ankles, however, were a disappointment—a little too broad. As for the rest. . . ."

He bunched his bejewelled fingers together and, lifting up his hand, threw his fingers open, at the same time screwing up his thick lips and making a noise like a kiss.

" Persik ! " (a peach), he said, and looked about him with a large display of happiness on his massive features.

" I motored down to the country house on Friday evening, had dinner, and played bridge afterwards with Mrs. Z——, her husband and another woman. Mrs. Z—— wore a beautiful pink crêpe de chine robe, carried a pink peony at her waist, and never stopped waving her hand through the air. Above her wedding-ring she wore a very fine emerald, an oblong stone like a crystallized caterpillar. There is a secret understanding among the English upper classes that if a woman wishes to open an intrigue with a man, she attracts his attention to the outstanding jewel on her finger by waving it before him artfully, laying her hand on his arm or placing her finger on her lips meditatively. One has to be in the country some time before one learns the intricacies of this lovers' language. I noticed the waving of the emerald ring, but didn't know at the time what it meant.

" We went to our bedrooms about eleven o'clock.

The Homes of the Mighty (*Petrograd*)

I had just come back from the bathroom and was standing in my silk dressing-gown when I heard a tap at the door. I said: 'Come in', thinking it was the manservant. The door opened and Mrs. Z—— (he gave the exact, very well-known name) entered. She wore embroidered yellow slippers and a silk kimono covered with humming birds and lotus flowers. Her beautiful hair was done in plaits down her back. 'Come right in!' I said. Quite needless, however, for she was in the room and locked the door before I could get the words out. 'So you understood my emerald message?' she said, holding up her dear little bejewelled hand for me to kiss. . . .

"I left on the following Monday morning, having thanked my charming hostess for her most delightful entertainment.

"About six months afterwards I was walking in Hyde Park and suddenly ran across Mrs. Z——. She was as charming as ever, wore a green hobble skirt and carried a sunshade. She beamed on me as though she was delighted to see me again. I bent over her hand to kiss it, and, noticing the emerald ring, I said to her by way of a happy reminder: 'The dear little love-messenger! Do you remember the happy times we had at B——? Will they ever come again?' To my utter astonishment she drew back suddenly, waved her green sunshade round with a violent sweep and snapped out: 'A gentleman never mentions those things.' And with that she turned and left me. There's a case of Puritanism!"

The Blue Steppes

The end of the table where he was holding court shook with merriment.

"But if she had only known, she would have realized that all I remembered of her was the emerald ring and a little blue wart two inches from her hip. . . ."

Since my return to England I have seen Mrs. Z—— several times, seen, too, the emerald "love-messenger", and wondered terribly whether she had any suspicion that I knew of the little blue wart two inches from the hip. I feel quite sure, however, that she has reformed and I hope there will be no flutter in the marital dovecotes of Mayfair, nor any undue searchings for a little blue wart.

Other experiences were related by Prince Drouki with that total "emancipation" peculiar to Russia, but more I will not divulge. This one is sufficient to point its own moral.

When I came back from the South of Russia and a visit to Count Clémétieff's estate, I found difficulty in getting a room at my hotel, which was full of officers. Count Clémétieff very kindly placed at my disposal a room in one of the houses adjoining his palace. He owned several houses round about where he offered accommodation to officers and friends arriving from the country or the front. I had just a few weeks to spare before setting out for England by a long and tedious journey through Finland, Sweden and Norway. I determined to see as much of the Russian Opera as I could and take a sip of the cup of revelry which was overflowing on all sides.

The Homes of the Mighty (Petrograd)

The day after I took up my residence in the house adjoining Count Clémétieff's palace, a beautiful lady appeared. She wore a war-nurse's grey costume with a white nun's-veiling over her head. It was in November 1916. A powdering of snow lay on the roofs and whitened the tops of the street lamps. I had just had breakfast and was reading the *Novoe Vremya* by the drawing-room window, looking out occasionally at the ice-floes sailing down the Neva and leaping now and again on one another's backs in the strong current. A door somewhere down one of the numerous corridors of the house slammed, and shortly after the beautiful lady appeared. She tripped across the Aubusson carpet with little trim steps and a swirl of her grey alpaca skirt. Radiant and linnet-voiced, she burst in upon me with a battery of charm.

"Now look here! you've got to make yourself thoroughly at home here. Don't stand on any Chinese ceremonies. Do exactly as you please and make yourself as cosy and happy as though you were in your own home or on your honeymoon. Akh!"

She sighed and turned to look out of the window at the ice-floes heralding the approach of winter and the freezing of the river.

"How time flies!" she added, dropping into the chair I pulled up for her. She pointed to the large clock on a Louis XV bureau depicting a marble Apollo and Venus in mutual approach, while underneath was written in golden letters: "Carpe Diem".

"Only nine o'clock," I said. "But whom have I the pleasure of addressing?"

She smiled and held out an elegant gold cigarette case with a delicate hand.

"Have one," she said. "We shall be friends, I hope. I'm Count Clémétieff's daughter. You've already met my sister, haven't you? I've been helping the British doctors that have come over. Wonderful men! Strong, healthy, such muscles! But oh! they are all so much alike. Like peas. No soul! no originality! One always knows what they are going to say before they open their mouths. It must be very dull for their wives. Do they have wives, these shaven British? Neither blood nor love seems to move them. Sometimes I think they haven't hearts of flesh and blood in their big breasts, but just iron pendulums like a grandfather's clock. Tick-tock! You hear the beat but it has no soul, no life! Akh! One could die from such a life!"

I wondered why this outburst so early in the morning and so soon in our acquaintance. I knew she was married, from common knowledge, but saw that she wore no wedding-ring.

"I suppose you will be leaving to join your husband," I said tentatively.

"Him? Oh, he's down at the front. A dreadfully spoilt one! He won't have me down there. Says I get in his way. He's twenty years older than me. Gaga already. No doubt he's having a merry time. They are all having a merry time in the rear of the army. Here in Petrograd, too, it is merry. Everyone is making the most of life. One must. Time won't wait. Tick-tock, tick-tock, it goes on like an endless funeral march. But one must have courage. One must neither think of the past nor of the future. Just be merry to-day. That's all. Do you love Maeterlinck? I adore him. He says it so well :

> "'Les autres jours sont déjà las,
> Les autres jours ont peur aussi,
> Les autres jours neviendront pas,
> Les autres jours mourront aussi,
> Nous aussi nous mourrons ici.'"

" I haven't read all his works," I declared.

" Then you must," she replied, going to a small table and bringing back a green, calf-bound volume. " Here are his poems."

" Thank you, I will read them to-night," I replied.

" To-night ? " she repeated. " What are you doing to-night ? "

" I'm going to the opera."

" I'm going to the ballet, but you must come with me afterwards for the Islands. It's sure to be amusing. The Grand Dukes P—— and M—— and Prince Upoff will be there. Some wonderful Chinese jugglers are going to give a show and Caucasian dancers will perform. It's all at a beautiful villa on the Islands."

Needless to say, I went. The Chinese jugglers juggled, the Caucasian dancers danced, the gypsy band twanged and sang their passionate songs, alternating love-lorn melancholy and dismal contemplation of the grave with shouts of wild delight and fiery raptures. Waiters flitted about with champagne and the inevitable caviare. The Grand Dukes looked massively happy, smiled occasionally and talked without end. The pick of the evening was a dance by a dusky Tartar Siberian woman who wriggled about with two large snakes twined round her waist.

Everything was done with tolerable decorum, the Grand Dukes were fairly reserved in their pawings of the two actresses they brought with them, holding their hands occasionally with tenderest devotion. One of them has since become a Grand Duchess, so that these fond caresses must have been symptoms of a genuine affection.

I left about two o'clock and went home. Personally, I should have been quite satisfied with attendance at the opera and a quiet reading before going to bed. But the cult of " wild sensations " was the vogue in Russia.

During the night I was awakened by the sound of the bedroom door creaking. The room was in total darkness, so I was unable to discover who the intruder was. I heard footsteps coming towards the bed. Not being familiar with ghosts or housebreakers, I slipped out of bed by the side against the wall and hid underneath.

Somebody patted the bed all over and then a woman's voice muttered : " There's a surprise. No doubt, he's already deceiving ! Who can it be ? "

She went through a list of names, but being able to settle on none, gave up the task and retired.

The Homes of the Mighty (*Petrograd*)

As soon as she was gone, I came out from my hiding-place and secured the door, which was keyless, by tying the doorknobs with a towel. No further disturbance occurred.

Next day I spent about town and returned about midnight. Having taken a bath, I slipped on my dressing-gown and proceeded through the dark suite of rooms towards my own. As I came towards the one before the last, I was surprised to see a faint light glowing tremulously. I thought it might be the lamp before the corner ikon customary to each room. Perhaps the servant had lighted it for some pious purpose. Entering the room, which was nothing but a recess in the corridor, I was surprised to see a bright-swathed figure reclining on a divan underneath the hanging blue lamp, while an odour of burning sandalwood pervaded the atmosphere. I was somewhat taken aback, as I had some personal belongings swinging over my arm and was not prepared to face one of the fair sex. I saw that it was Madame Viedlovski, the daughter of Count Clémétieff, dreaming of bliss by the flickering light of the tiny blue lamp, and burning fragrances in a little porphyry vase. I went straight ahead without stopping to look at her more than once.

"Don't be too hasty!" she called out. "Here are some wonderful opiums. Or if you like some cocaine. Try them. It is like being in paradise."

I waited for no more, but slipped along to my room and fastened the towel round the door knobs as tight as my agitation allowed me.

The Blue Steppes

Next day I told Countess Clémétieff that I was going back to the hotel.

"I know why," she said. "You are probably frightened by my daughter. Alas! the younger generation have all sorts of odd ideas. But don't go to the hotel. There is plenty of room in the house opposite. My son had it for his flat before he married. There is only a young Cossack officer, a friend of ours, who sleeps there at present."

So I quitted the house with the beautiful lady and the blue hanging lamp and went to the house of the Cossack. The latter was a tall, handsome young man of thirty or so and was just up from the Galician front. He carried about in his pocket Poe's *Tales of Mystery* and quoted from it with an ardour that was only matched by its frequency. He was extremely well cultivated, though he loved the wild life of the steppes and forests and was an admirable companion when he was not on the spree, which was rather frequent. His chief disadvantage was a fondness for firing pistols. He wore two always loaded on the hips of his pleated Circassian uniform. On the morning after my first night in the apartment, he flung open the folding doors that separated our bedrooms and called out, while I lay in bed: "Don't trouble! I'm just going to have my morning practice."

And before I had time to answer or wipe the dreams from my drowsy eyes, a pistol shot plugged the wall just above my bed. I looked up and saw a round disc with bull's-eye and circles fastened

The Homes of the Mighty (Petrograd)

half-way up the wall. He fired away for about ten minutes with consummate skill, hitting the bull's-eye every time. When I was duly impressed, he threw a cake of Pears' soap on to the bed and telling me to make a tent with my knees and place the soap on top, declared he would send it flying. However, I hopped out of bed and took the soap with me to the bathroom.

When I left the house a few weeks later, he had gone back to the merry front, while I set out on the long, wearisome journey to England to tell people of the state of Russia and the impending revolution. But no one believed it. Perhaps they didn't wish to, having their irons already well in the fire. . . .

. . . . .

After the revolution, Count Clémétieff's wine cellars were sacked by the mob and later on the whole house with all its priceless treasures was burnt down, because the revolutionaries, bent on confiscating the Count's famous collection of gold and silver plate, declared that he had hidden it in the walls!

Chapter XIII

THE HOMES OF THE MIGHTY (*MOSCOW*)

I

THEY WERE a great family, the Torozoffs. Their name spelt wealth and scores of factories, their palaces made the glory of modern Moscow. One hundred years ago the foundations of their immense fortunes had been laid by their common ancestor, a pious peasant owned by a Prince Dolgorouki and blessed in his poverty with vision and twenty-four sons. Such a quiverful of heavenly benedictions might have ruined a family for ages. There was no birth control in those days, nor indeed would pious Ivan Torozoff have smiled on such an impiety. He took both his poverty and his sons with blessings and set them to work. At first he had a hand loom, wove coarse fustian for the peasant women and then, daring all, sold his cow, ordered his grown-up sons to sell their cows, pooled the money and bought an English loom. Matters developed apace till all the twenty-four sons and their wives were at work at looms in their little wooden huts. In 1915, when I met one of his millionaire descendants, the family was the wealthiest in Russia.

THE COUNTRY HOUSE OF M. TOROZOFF.

[To face p. 198.

The Homes of the Mighty (Moscow)

Timofey Torozoff was the uncle of some student and officer friends of mine. When I went to stay with them for a few weeks in the summer they were living in a wooden châlet on their uncle's estate. His roomy house, built in a mixed Flemish, Gothic and French style, stood on a green cliff-like bank of the river Moscow in the neighbourhood of the ancient, railwayless, tramless, busless, sewerless, noiseless, delightful little town of Svenigorod. Peace and vast spaces reigned all around. The estate was approached through a leafy, odorous, dreamy forest, miles long, through hedgeless meadowland, miles long, through lark-sung fields of waving golden corn, so far-flung that yonder peasant in his cart on the sandy road seemed like a pin-head on a cloth of gold. Just a row of neat wooden izbas, with carved and painted lattices, stretched along either side of the grassy track before the gates of the garden, while an ancient white church lifted its speckled domes, golden crosses and dove-cote belfry against the blue sky. Enchanting spot!

"When shall I have the pleasure of meeting your uncle?" I asked my friends.

"One never knows," they replied. "He dislikes company. He is fifty-five, a bachelor, and prefers the consolation of art. Sometimes he plays tennis, but very rarely. We may meet him one day in the park. He walks about sometimes."

However, I was destined to meet Timofey Torozoff much sooner than they expected. Their father, who was an important Minister in the Government, suddenly arrived for a few days' seclusion in order to make up his mind about the policy of the Cabinet. (He resigned, in fact, having fallen into disgrace with the Empress.) My room was wanted, so it was decided that Uncle Timofey should be requested to allow me to sleep in the large Gothic house.

We met the millionaire in one of the shady pine-walks skirting the precipitous bank of the river. He carried his hat in his hand and was panting like a great St. Bernard, for the day was sultry and he was corpulent. A pleasant face, tipped with a small imperial, smiled benignly at us, while a mellow voice, monosyllabic (or the nearest approach to that in polysyllabic Russian), rather inclined to be plaintive, mingled a greeting with a mention of the weather. It was obvious this man of vast wealth was rather shy. On the other hand, his name was known throughout Russia as a generous benefactor to all good and noble causes. He had built and equipped hospitals, founded almshouses, chairs of learning, museums, clubs, and was one of the leading members of the Moscow Society for the Encouragement of Horse-racing. A true and independent judge of art, he never waited with his millions to purchase a picture only when it had become an object of commercial value or when the artist was " established ". He never waited to hear what verdict the critics would proclaim. He was satisfied entirely with his own. It must have been good, for every one of his artistic possessions was afterwards confiscated as art treasure by the Soviet. Yet it was he who

The Homes of the Mighty (Moscow)

helped the poor, unrecognized artists to live and produce. He also devoted much of his wealth and energy to the fostering of rustic art among the peasantry, and a large establishment under his name was set up in Moscow on the Leontovski Pereulok, though I regret to say that the majority of the patterns, *genre Russe*, distributed among the peasants were imported from Germany !

In spite of all this social excellency, this ardent desire to benefit every class of the population, he was evidently a lonely man, indeed, a tortured man. Some indication of the nature of his suffering was soon forthcoming.

He had hardly given his consent to my sleeping in the Gothic mansion, when a little, chubby, white-flannelled man with a Punch-like expression came swinging down the pine-walk, waving his straw hat and walking-stick and bursting with melody, singing snatches from " The Dollar Princess ". Timofey Torozoff turned and fled. Discreetly, of course. The little " Punch " man came up and was introduced as Doctor Fantz, the millionaire's personal medical attendant.

Anyone less " professional " in mood or manner it would be hard to find. He banged his straw hat on the back of his head, thrust his walking-stick between his legs and hopped over it, first one leg, then the other, said impossible things, laughed uproariously at them, made funny horse noises with his sensuous red lips, and caught his neighbour every minute or so by the arm or shoulder with his flabby, diamond-studded hand.

"Couldn't your uncle find a better man than that?" I asked afterwards, when my friends apologized for the exhibition.

"He's had him ten years already and pays him 20,000 roubles (£2,000) a year. And the funniest thing of all is when Uncle Timofey is unwell. He sends for another doctor. Doctor Fantz, of course, doesn't mind that. He has his wife and family, his villa here, and a house in town built for him by my uncle next door to his own; he draws his big salary every month at the office, dines and wines on the pick of my uncle's larder and wine-cellar and uses one of the motor-cars almost exclusively for himself."

"How does your uncle manage to keep him?"

"Simply because Doctor Fantz has persuaded him that he is likely any moment to drop dead. He distrusts the doctor, though he knows he has some trivial heart complaint. So when he feels unwell, he goes to another doctor in order to be persuaded the trouble isn't too serious. But he must always have Doctor Fantz near him and will never go a day without having him somewhere in the neighbourhood, in case he shouldn't be able to go to the other doctor quick enough. You see, the doctor has persuaded him to one thing about himself, and that only his own attachment can save him. So he is in perpetual revolt against it. But we Russians are terrible fatalists. There is always the chance of Doctor Fantz being right. It is just as though he had seen the number thirteen written on his brow and was expecting every moment to hear Doctor Fantz pronounce the fatal words : ' I told you so ! ' "

" Then it is nothing but an idea ? "

" What will you ? We Russians live on ideas and must always have one great *idée fixe* to which we enslave our souls."

I slept in the long, panelled room assigned to me, saw the golden moon creep up over the white tower of a distant church beyond the slumbering heath and sparkling waters of the winding river, heard the piping calls of the peewits in the fields of corn and smelt the oaten fragrance wafted through the open windows on the warm night air. About midnight the high wailing of the village maidens and the cries of the peasants trailing their fishing nets along the river gave place to the perfect quiet of the short July night. I sank into the arms of sleep. At break of dawn I was awakened by groans, horrid, long-drawn groans that ran through the dark, panelled house like the echoes of something sinister. I heard the scuttling of slippered feet along the corridor, the banging of a door, a low voice from afar, then silence. The groans ceased. It was my first night in the great stone house, in the house of the millionaire who shunned society. Gruesome as the groans seemed to me in the cold stillness of the breaking dawn, I wearied of waiting for their renewal and dropped off to sleep again.

In the morning I was awakened by the sound of a singing voice. It came up from the grassy terrace before the house and streamed into the musty room together with the golden sunshine pouring in through the open windows. I heard, too, the larks leaping up on the light breeze over the cornfields. I sprang out of bed and went to the window to breathe the fragrant air and see the morning singer. No doubt it was a beautiful peasant-girl, carrying her flashing scythe and pouring out her heart in song as she swung along to the reaping fields. Bucolic sweetness always enchanted me. . . .

I looked out of the window and stood stock still, my eyes enchanted with another vision. Over the broad green sward leading down to the river walked a woman. Her back was turned to the house. On her left arm swung a bathing towel. Singing and tripping with an air of morning bliss, she was clothed in grace alone. . . .

The banging of a window and a door caught in the draught told me there were other observers of this biblical spectacle. The swaying, singing form disappeared over the brink of the river's bank and a few moments later bubbles rose to the surface of the water.

It was Rebecca, the raven-locked wife of Doctor Fantz. Every morning, during the whole three weeks of my stay at Spenskoe, I was awakened by her morning song and greeted whenever I went to the open window by the vision of her pale form swaying joyfully in its primal grace across the green sward to the river's bank. The only variation in this matutinal idyll was when Doctor Fantz, leaping like a satyr, gleamed brownish and grotesque by her lissom side.

The Homes of the Mighty (Moscow)

The groans continued likewise by night. They were, I gathered, the property of the ferret-eyed manservant. He was darkly suspicious of anyone entering the house and did not conceal his annoyance at my being allowed to sleep there. He, too, like his master, suffered from heart trouble, and his nightly attacks were skilfully administered to by Doctor Fantz, his fears and sufferings allayed by that learned worthy, and the millionaire lord of all nightly impressed by the horrors of heart trouble and the admirable skill of his doctor in fighting them.

Little more might have been suspected had not Timofey Torozoff met us in the park with tears in his eyes and voice. " Look here ! " he said, holding out a piece of paper. " Is it not monstrous ? I rarely touch a morsel of meat, yet here is the monthly bill for meat which the cook has just presented. 4,259 roubles (£425) for meat for myself alone ! Four thousand pounds of meat consumed by me in the space of one month ! No wonder I am so unbearably corpulent and people marvel when I tell them I am on thin diet in order to take down my bulk ! Alas ! What's to be done ! Every month it is the same. Every bill I receive is written out in the same proportion."

We left him, clad in white, hurrying along the breezy walk on the high bank of the river, fanning himself with his panama and moaning to the bee-loud limes.

" Why doesn't he dismiss the chef ? " I asked my friend.

"With us it is so," he returned. "One fears to get a worse one in his place. To-day we wanted strawberries from the gardener, but he sends all to the market in Moscow. What my uncle requires for his own table he has to pay for. The Oopravlayooshtchi (steward) is just as bad. The gardener, the chef, the steward have all built great blocks of flats in Moscow. My uncle does nothing. It is always so in Russia. It is expected. Everybody steals. One complains a little, but one pays just the same. It isn't worth while to resist. It was always so. The next might be worse."

So the colossal stealing went on week after week and the colossal bills were presented to the unhappy millionaire and paid. Of course, he protested. But words have no effect in Russia, while no one seemed to have energy or perhaps faith enough to act.

Uncle Timofey consoled himself with the fostering of art, barring music, which, he told me, made him want to wail just like a dog whenever he heard anything but the human voice. I fancy the morning song of the doctor's wife as she swayed past his bedroom window must have been a pre-concerted attack on the one chord in his heart that responded to the charm of music.

Himself a most agreeable man, he made the stay at Spenskoe a dream of delight, placing horses, motor-cars and carriages at the disposal of his nephews and supplying their table with his choicest wines.

The Homes of the Mighty (*Moscow*)

His servants were all well treated, in fact, as will have been gathered, they treated themselves extremely well and their employer very badly. When the revolution came they behaved still worse.

The chauffeur used to send in fabulous bills for repairs and working expenses, all of which were paid. By the time the revolution came he must have had quite a fortune. Under the Kerensky régime, when every man was striking for higher wages, Torozoff's chauffeur struck too, demanding enormous wages. It was nothing short of blackmail, for when I went to pay a visit to the poor millionaire, I noticed a large piece of paper nailed to the entrance gates. In large red letters there appeared the words:

"CHAUFFEUR ON STRIKE
JOB UNDER BOYCOTT."

Timofey Torozoff told me with distress in his voice: "He demanded such unheard-of wages. How could I pay, when all the workers of my factories are asking such wages that the business can only be run at a loss? Already I am obliged to sell some of my property in order to carry on this establishment and keep one group of factories going. One has to ruin one factory to save another. The folk are blind, led on by fanatics. I told him he would have to find another master, but you see what he does. He threatens to shoot the first man that applies. They are all like that!"

He waved his hand downwards hopelessly, heaving a sigh.

"Prodajhnie!" (venable) "unconscionables!"

The man stayed, but when the Bolshevists confiscated the car, his master made no complaint and considered himself so much the richer and freer.

As for Spenskoe, the beautiful estate on the banks of the Moscow river, the thieving steward and gardener with one or two other employees declared themselves communists and established themselves with their families in the Gothic house, and monopolizing the land against the pretensions of the local peasants, sold the produce for their own benefit. When, owing to lack of labour and cash, they were unable to cultivate the greater part of it, they refused to let any of the peasants till it and threatened to massacre anyone who tried. But in this they were hardly to be blamed, for the essence of Bolshevism as a propaganda for the abolition of private ownership is to inflame the acquisitive and possessive instincts of the non-possessing and to attract those who smell a fine chance to acquire Nabob's vineyard.

II

Another Moscow millionaire in whose house I was privileged to dwell for a short while was Ivan Shookin. His benefactions to the town of Moscow were a household word. To his generosity were due the Alexander III Museum and the wonderful collection of French post-impressionist paintings in the Annunciation Alley. Heir to millions at the age of eighteen, he had devoted his life to the welfare of his workers, the health of the town

The Homes of the Mighty (Moscow)

population, the fostering of learning and the arts. He owned two houses in Moscow, one in which he hung his collection of Matisse, Cézanne, Van Gogue, Picasso and similar paintings and another in which he dwelt with his family. Every day he hurried forth to the former in order to be near his precious paintings, to show them to visitors and sing their glories. Thursdays and Sundays were free days to the public, yet he would still be there to answer questions and see to the happiness of his general guests.

I went to live in his house in the early months of 1918. The Bolshevists were in the saddle and lashing about them with the sword. Ivan Shookin's one absorbing interest was to save his collection of art treasures from the Bolshevists. In those days the policy of the Soviet rulers towards the relics of "bourgeois" art had not been definitely decided. The violent section were clamorous for the destruction of all "bourgeois" relics, as pernicious reminders of the old capitalistic system and culture, apt to divert the eyes of the newly generated communist citizens from their actual misery to the lost charms of the old order, to foster evil comparisons, whereas the new and glorious proletarian culture had not yet appeared save in the hideous forms of lewd Futurism and ugly Asiatic Epsteinisms. Much slashing of pictures had already taken place and there were not wanting egregious heroes and heroines who were ready to "deepen the revolution" by destroying every vestige of heretical "bourgeois art". While the great battle was waging among the Bolshevists, the various professors and learned people put all their forces together " to save the treasures of Russian culture ", laying aside all their political prejudices, they offered their services to the Soviet. Lenin saw the advantage of finding some sort of working basis with these influential circles and welcomed them. In this way the struggle for the preservation of Russia's " bourgeois relics " was successful.

Ivan Shookin was one of the leaders of this movement of rescue. He was allowed to look after his collection, imparting his knowledge and enthusiasm to all his visitors. But he was not so comfortable in the house where his family lived. Already various Soviet officials had turned their avid eyes upon it. To obviate the disaster of being turned out, Ivan Shookin did what was then a common practice among people with large houses. Rather than have Bolshevists foisted upon them, they invited respectable foreigners to occupy some of the rooms and safeguard them against Soviet intrusion by nailing a consular certificate of protection on to the door. For this purpose, Ivan Shookin extended to me an invitation to occupy a couple of rooms in his house. The offer was very opportune. I had just lost my abode in a friend's house to a gang of Soviet officials, a fearful mixture of sexes and morals, that not all the disinfectants of the world would purify. Indeed, they invaded the house with a blatant contempt for all " bourgeois " morality.

The Homes of the Mighty (*Moscow*)

My stay with Ivan Shookin was very agreeable to begin with. Being a man of much personal charm, aged about sixty-three and full of interest in life, he still made an effort to do the honours of traditional Russian hospitality to distinguished foreigners staying in the town. Artists and actors still came to his *soirées* as in the palmy days before the revolution. The great feasting table would be set at the bottom of the high banqueting hall, ablaze with a myriad wax tapers and loaded with exquisite food. Even in those dark days of famine and distress, he was able to get rich delicacies by paying well. The secret lay in keeping in touch with minor Soviet officials. While Lenin and a few of the doctrinaire leaders led strenuous lives boiling the great Russian nation in the cauldron of Communism, the greater part of their adepts were bent on feasting themselves on the confiscated riches while the sovereign people starved and was shot into submission.

So many of them were anxious to pile up fortunes abroad and were sending money to Sweden and Switzerland so that their share of the Dictatorship of the Proletariat might be safe in the event of its downfall. Though money had been officially deprived of its value, these ardent communists were always glad to get as much as they could and would sell food and wines from the confiscated cellars, or the pick of the country's produce reserved for Soviet officials.

Ivan Shookin availed himself of this delightful trait of Communism. Whenever his guests asked him where he got his choice wines and caviare from during such bad times, he used to answer, " From the lilies of the field ". Such was the term among many people in Moscow to designate the Soviet officials, who toiled not, neither did they spin, yet Solomon in all his glory was not arrayed as one of these. In fact, they affected leather jackets and were provided with the best of everything before all others, feeding the people with promises.

To the house flocked many Russian actors and actresses who were being superseded at the theatres by Hebrew artists. So intense was this Hebrew solidarity that hardly a Russian artist was allowed to remain. Apart from this, most Russian theatrical artists retained the old " bourgeois " conceptions of art and were averse from accepting the new version, which was directed against all that was dearest to them in their nation and national consciousness, scruples which Hebrews naturally did not share. And it was a curious and illuminating commentary on actual happenings, that wherever the old Russian national spirit and consciousness was suppressed, the Hebrew came out on top.

Most of these stricken artists were anxious to get abroad, away from the sickening sight of the massacre of their dearest national sentiments. It was strange to notice that, when it was too late, the intelligentsia seemed to repent of its former a-nationalism, a-patriotism, a-morality and vague socialistic, international, amorphous, hysterical

The Homes of the Mighty (*Moscow*)

mentality. Belated as this awakening from vain visions was, it came like a staggering blow between the eyes. The stars they had contemplated with such ardour fell in the dust about them. Millions trekked across the border, while hundreds of thousands were wiped off the face of the earth by the terrible monster they had so long nursed unwittingly in their bosom, bred with their own persistent negations and aspirations towards the universal.

Besides artists, actors and literateurs, who frequented the house of Ivan Shookin, there were a good number of foreigners, chiefly members of the diplomatic missions. One stout Swedish baron, whose name I neglected to note, enlivened one remarkable *soirée* by telling hair-raising tales of his lion-hunting expedition in Africa in company with Prince William of Sweden He related his story with the utmost solemnity. When he came to the moment when the lions were heard roaring, he threw out his portly, diamond-studded chest, took an immense breath of air, and bulging out his cheeks, eyes and lips, made such fearful noises that the young ladies blew their noses; whether to hide their terror or to add to it, I know not. The story, I may add, was told in rugged German, so that every time the baron pronounced the diphthong "au", he did it with such a mighty discharge of the "ah-oo" that one almost heard the echo of the roaring lions without need of further demonstration.

To counter this enormous success, Ivan Shookin

himself related the thrilling episodes of his journey to Mount Ararat and his sojourn at the ancient monastery of Saint Catherine at Sinai. It was interesting to note the difference in outlook of the two story-tellers; the Swedish lion-hunter having no eye or ear for the beauties of nature and losing his soul to the roar of the lion, while Ivan Shookin lost himself in wonderful descriptions of the golden, burning sands of the desert turning to rose-pink at sunset, of the jingling bells of the camels and caravans, of the beautiful mosaics and services in the ancient monastery of St. Catherine, and finally, with one great sweep of human feeling, of the sad plight of a young monk who had looked after him and had confided to him his sufferings. He had been a lawyer in Athens, killed a man in a love affair and, filled with repentance, had vowed his life to the service of God at the ancient monastery situated down a far-off gorge in the midst of the arid desert. The heat was so intense that his physical and moral sufferings were scarcely bearable.

"I stood with him on the roof of the guest-house," Ivan Shookin related in his succulent voice. "We watched the gorgeous rays of the scorching sun die down over the quivering sand of the desert. The sky hung above like an immense sapphire bubble, and, with the passing of the sun, the whole earth seemed to swell upwards like a vast, rising vapour tinged with a melting pink that was lovely beyond compare. From the turret of the church came the melodious swaying of the

The Homes of the Mighty (Moscow)

bells and the strong voices of monks singing the preparatory hymn. There were shouts in the hot, extended air from the camp where the camels shook their tinkling bells. My handsome guide covered his face in his hands and heaved a deep sigh. 'You go to-morrow,' he said, 'back to the world I have abandoned, the world of merry sounds, laughter and love, of battle and struggle. But I shall remain here in the scorching solitude of the desert, where nothing of the old life follows me but its dreams. My God! It is hardly possible for human flesh and blood. Always I think of the past, of my lost hopes and ambitions, my terrible wrong-doing. And all the time the image of her for whom I sinned comes back to torture me. She hovers about me always. She is in the rays of the sun. She burns me with her kisses. She is in the cool of the garden shade, in the refreshment of the water from the deep well, speaking to me of the quieter bliss she wove for me. But I will not go back. I will stay here, bearing this cross. Perhaps in the unseen scheme of things there is more wisdom in this sacrifice than if I returned to the ways of love and possession which have already wrought so much harm.'"

The lion-hunter showed signs of restlessness, being more concerned with the roaring of earthly lions than of the heavenly adversary. He hastily proposed a song and offered to provide the voice himself. We were fearfully startled at this announcement, having still in our ears the echo of his recent attempt to imitate a lion's roar. But none of us would deny that it had provided us with a very enjoyable moment. So we applauded the Swedish baron's proposal. He forthwith went to the grand piano, chose " Der Erlkönig " from a pile of notes, called up the accompanist, heaved his portly, diamond-studded chest and let go with such dash and volume of sound that we expected to see the ceiling come rattling down. Instead of airy phantoms, there must have been lions on all sides of the unfortunate Erlking, for the baron let fly at them with such terrific blasts that the very Lion of Araby would have slunk home at the sound with his tail between his legs. Nevertheless, we applauded heartily and asked for more. Which the baron very obligingly provided. And all the while, Communism and Leninism were in power outside, wreaking their odious evil on poor, tortured humanity. But it was useless to sentimentalize about it. The cabarets and theatres never once ceased to function, even when men were being shot in thousands and the populace was starving and cowed. I think at the Last Day there will be thousands who will find amusement of some sort while waiting their turn to be judged.

After the third song of the obliging baron a little untoward incident occurred. Ivan Shookin's second wife had formerly been a school teacher, divorced from a Frenchman, who was among the guests. Thinking the baron needed a chair after his tempestuous exertions, she offered him one as he stood bending over the pile of notes and selecting another song.

The Homes of the Mighty (Moscow)

"No, no, I don't want it!" he exclaimed very abruptly in a rugged tone of voice, and went on with his search. Madame Shookin went off into an adjoining room. Presently some women went in to her.

Her little fluffy head was all dishevelled, her lips running red. I looked in. Madame Shookin was sitting on the divan, weeping.

"How could he speak to me like that?" she sobbed. "I wanted to look after his comfort. Why was he so rude, so abrupt, so unfeeling?"

"Madame," I ventured to suggest, "he has been so used to dealing with lions and relating about them so often that he must always have them on the brain. Take it as a compliment. No lion-hunter likes to be offered comfort by a lady. The idea of comfort is repulsive to a big-game hunter. One must take it for flattery that he speaks to a lady as he would to a lion."

Smiles shone through the welling tears and the little lady smoothed out her ruffled locks, opened her satchel and readjusted the line of her lips. Consolation bloomed in her eyes and laughter lurked roguishly in her slender throat once more. And to roll back every cloud of sorrow from her vision, the booming voice of the lion-hunting baron surged tumultuously into the room from the resounding hall. It was as though a terrific avalanche of rocks and boulders and gurgling waters had been let loose from the top of a stormy mountain:

> " Ich komme vom Gebirge he-e-E-E-rrr,
> Es dä-ä-Ä-Ä-mpft das Tha-a-A-A-l,
> Es brau-oo-oo-OO-st das Me-e-E-E-rrr. . . ."

The little lady sank back on to the divan overcome with emotion. " He's so powerful ! " she exclaimed between fits of weeping laughter. " He makes something go wobbly inside of me. He touches such a funny chord in my heart."

So, recovering from her fit of tears and resentment, she went back to her guests in the hall full of laughter and chatter.

After a few performances on the piano by a well-known artist, it was decided to sit down to the feast at the long table laden with flaming tapers, a hissing samovar, and dishes of salads, *zakuski* and succulent meats. Being carnival time, the customary *blini* or pancakes, some made with chopped fish, some with minced meat or chopped onion, were served with melted butter or cream sauce. Then began the Russian custom of stuffing oneself with *blini* in order to beat every other person at table in the number consumed.

"Five ! Ten ! Fifteen, twenty, thirty ! " they shouted, glowing and swelling and oozing with pride of accomplishment.

No one ate less than ten, after which they consumed the delicacies surreptitiously bought from hands that should have served them to the Dictators of the Proletariat. There was a peculiar thrill in the knowledge that one was consuming caviare that should have entered the communistic mouth of a commissar whose lips still oozed with promises

The Homes of the Mighty (Moscow)

of paradise for the people, and whose hands were eager for the first fruits.

Such festive evenings were rare, however, in this once famous house, and depended on the will and cupidity of the Soviet officials who supplied the good things. Bribery, peculation, favouritism, underhand dealings and treachery were still more rife since the overthrow of Tsardom. That was only natural, for it was by stirring up the cupidity and envy of the masses in a wholesale manner that Lenin made his bid for power, and it was only too obvious that the destruction of the old private ownership did nothing but over-excite the lust for possession in those who had the new chance. It became the rage to get what one could out of the communistic, property-abolishing order and hide it away in expectation of the time when Sovietism will be as the memory of a hideous nightmare. Psychologically the attitude of most people was to get what one could out of the smashing and confiscating, and wait for the inevitable fall of Communism. For this reason there was a mad desire to get and hide Tsarist rouble notes in the belief that they alone would have a value after the return to normal conditions.

About the middle of 1918, the Soviet people began to harass Ivan Shookin in spite of the foreigners and their consular certificates. One day a young commissar arrived in the company of a rather pretty woman and demanded to look over the house. After a tour of inspection, he went back to Ivan Shookin's bedroom and said : " Clear out of this. I want this for me and my companion. Also the room adjoining."

Accordingly the rooms were relinquished. The commissar came in, occupied the bedroom with his companion and made himself at home. The commissar was somewhat surly, but the young woman, a Serbian Jewess, was pleasant though contemptuous of all " bourgeois " codes. Unfortunately she left after a week or so, and her place as " companion " was taken by another woman, whose loud, toneless voice hooted like a horrible motor-horn throughout the house. Occupying the best bedroom and study, she made herself communistically objectionable. Her nose, like her harsh voice, was always in the air.

" Bourjhooika ! " she would say disdainfully to Madame Shookin. " Bloodsucker ! We will show you what it is to drink our blood ! " All the claptrap of the Communist rolled from her lips like the toads from the lips of the girl in the fairy tale.

" As for you English," she said, addressing me on the stairs, " a nation of dog's faces, that's what you are. But wait ! We will show you bloodthirsty English what strength is. A people of patriots, general-shopkeepers, and aristocratic working-men must be swept off the face of the earth. You have tortured the world too long with your moral airs and exploitations. We shall level you down a bit."

Whenever she passed me in the house, she would hold forth about the " English gang of dog-faces,

The Homes of the Mighty (Moscow)

shopkeepers and knightly working-men" (*shaika sobachikh mord, lavochnikov i rytzarskix rabochikh*). She used to roll the phrase off with great unction and contempt, especially the "knightly working-men", as though they were the epitome of all that was revolting to her communistic nature. Her contempt for knightliness was all the more vast because Russia was never within the orbit of the knightly aspirations of Medieval Europe and consequently had inherited none of its traditions or moral values. Only those who know the Russian language thoroughly and are conversant with Soviet Russia can realize the depth of the contempt which the Russian Communists entertain towards the British trade-unionists. This hatred and contempt comes from the fact that the British working-man does not see any utility or take any delight in throwing bombs about or smashing up what he gets his living by for the sake of something that is all in the air and likely to deprive him of his liberty, and what he has already. Being mostly doctrinaire theoreticians, the Communist leaders shot the trade-unionist leaders and the more virile type of working-man, especially after their demand for the continuation of the right to strike. Such a demand was dubbed "treason to the Socialistic State", and in order to convert the trade unions into a servile appendage of the Central Communist Bureau, the Soviet shot the leaders and men with private judgment. I was myself in prison with the men of the Prokhorov factory in Moscow and heard their protest against the destruction of the real trade unions before they were taken out to be shot.

As for the Soviet woman, with her constant stream of contempt and hatred, she was left severely alone by all the rest of the inhabitants of the house. However, she refused to let them alone. A difficulty arose of a very intimate nature. Ivan Shookin's bathroom was commandeered by these communistic personages. As the only other bath was out of order and no one could be got to mend it, we were all obliged to use Ivan Shookin's bathroom. It was a tiled construction sunk in the floor with ledges round the sides to sit or lie on.

None of us relished the necessity of using the bath after the commissar and his companion. Moreover, they were out-and-out Communists in everything. Ivan Shookin's house had always been a home of decency and respectability and had stood out against the wave of corruption which swept Russia long before the revolution. But he could do nothing to prevent the Communists from invading his home and bringing with them their morals and manners.

For one thing, none of us liked the necessity of having to put up with the offensive intrusion of free love into the home. Communists, of course, disclaim any respect for other people's views or feelings. Such things are labelled as " prejudice ", " bourgeois mentality ", and you have to have them knocked out of you.

The Homes of the Mighty (Moscow)

The young commissar had already changed his companion within ten days. Moreover, they used the bathroom communistically every night and morning and prevented others from getting an honest wash. One dared make no protest for fear of being thrown out into the street.

Now about this time (April 1918) a great stir was produced throughout Russia by the suggestions of several local Soviets for the nationalization of women. The newspapers were full of the subject. The Soviet of Saratoff decreed that a man could take any woman to wife and should pay her 250 roubles a month, the " marriage " to be terminated by dismissal. Similar decrees were issued by the Soviets at Pokrov, Vladimir, and at Svenigorod, near the estate of my friends on the Moscow river. Fortunately, in the latter place, the peasants and townsmen rose in revolt against the attack on their womenfolk and killed the ringleaders of the Soviet. (Accounts of these happenings may be read in the *Russkoe Slovo*, the *Moskovskiya Birjhevia Viedomosti* and the Soviet *Izvestia* during April-May 1918.)

There was naturally a great resentment among the intelligentsia, who began to see at last that there were indeed such things as sanctities in life and that their Nietzschean philosophy had led them astray. The excitement about this matter became acute, especially as a battle was raging within the Communist Party itself concerning the position of marriage in the Communist State. Private ownership having been abolished, it was maintained that no man could possess a wife under the old " bourgeois " conditions. Free love had always been a paramount plank in the Communists' platform and the downright section of the party, who stood for the full application of their principles and no mercy for old " bourgeois " prejudices, fought hard for the total abolition of any legal sanction for the union of the sexes. That was a matter to be left entirely to the wills of the citizens, to be arranged amongst themselves according to their pleasure. Men and women being on an equal footing and there being no longer any question of providing for a wife, maintaining her, or founding a family, marriage as an institution was to be abolished. Men and women were to come together at their caprice and whatever offspring they chanced to have would be taken over and brought up by the Communist State. There was to be no question of family life. These views were maintained by the consequential doctrinaires and the " deepeners of the revolution ", and although they started at once to apply them to actual life, it soon became evident that the State was utterly unable to carry the system out universally. Communists naturally lived together in the glory of free love, changing their partners according to their caprice and putting their children out into the State children's colonies founded on some of the confiscated estates. But even these were failures, and the Soviet found itself forced to rely on the private instincts and the " bourgeois " idea of love and parental affec-

The Homes of the Mighty (Moscow)

tion for the maintenance of the nation's children. In spite of all the high-sounding eloquence, the rosy visions, the snowstorm of Soviet decrees, nothing seemed to work out successfully on communistic lines. All that could be done was to maintain a model children's colony, a model farm, factory, hospital, works, school, etc., here and there throughout the vast land of Russia, where the communistic idea would be seen working out harmoniously. Naturally these "models" (*obraztsovie*) were maintained at the expense of the State, a sort of robbing Peter to dress up Paul, and they were especially cultivated and adorned for the benefit of foreign visitors. The model Communist "children's colonies" were so maintained even when the Soviet newspaper itself had to complain of the thousands of beggar children roaming about the country.

There was a loud section of the Communist Party which cried out for the nationalization of women on the ground that everything in the Communist State was for common service (*upotreblienie*) and nothing for keeping. And to prevent the unjust distribution of the more desirable women it was considered advisable to nationalize them. The idea was freely discussed, and as I have already mentioned, translated into the form of a Soviet decree in various localities. It was the natural outcome of the Communist theory, of the abolition of private ownership, the family, and "bourgeois" morality, of the sentiments of love and parental affection, and of the substitution of communal ownership, free intercourse, and the nationalization of the "services" and "commodities".

It can well be imagined how great was the outcry of Russia against this outrageous project. The intelligentsia, who for years had practised and preached sex-communism as the "latest dictum of science", recovered its head at last and woke up to the horror of seeing itself in the Soviet mirror with all the foul consequences of its advanced teaching and practices legally enthroned by thorough-going, consequential doctrinaires.

I sympathized with their revolt, but as I had often argued with them about the consequences of their views long before the revolution, I might have used that hideous phrase: "I told you so!"

Lenin and Trotsky, it appeared, were all for caution in applying their Communist theory to the country as a whole. To maintain the children of 120,000,000 peasants in children's colonies was obviously a fool's task. Private ownership in this case was much better. So that part of the Communist paradise was left to be practised on the children of the Communist caste, for whom the confiscated mansions and estates were set aside. In general the children of the workers and peasants were left to the private energies and affections of their parents with a good deal of starvation and misery in the bargain.

Nevertheless, the Soviet leaders destroyed the value of marriage by subtler means. They issued

The Homes of the Mighty (Moscow)

a decree whereby any man or woman could contract "marriage" or dissolve it by making a simple declaration before a commissar. This was a sop thrown out to the great majority of the people in whom the old idea of marriage still lingered pretty toughly. Marriage, however, as an institution was smashed. A man or woman could marry to-day and either of them could go round to the local commissar next morning and divorce his or her partner by just declaring: "I've done with her" (or him). In this way the prostitute picked up in the streets could be registered as a legal "wife" and "divorced" in the space of a few hours by all who cared to avail themselves of the "marriage" law. Most Communists believing in absolute free love did not trouble about this formality, though "bourgeois" respectability still held its sway over a good many and still counted for much among the vast majority of the population. In the house of Ivan Shookin, the young commissar who occupied the best rooms soon grew tired of his second "wife" and introduced a third.

This time the second did not leave. She still refused to go, although her "husband" told her he had declared her divorced before the local commissar, and had "married" the third woman. There were terrible ructions every evening when the commissar came home from his office.

Ivan Shookin naturally complained about the man having two wives in the house, but was told to swallow his bourgeois prejudices, which were no longer of any importance under Communism. He was very upset, for never before in his long life had he been obliged to live together with people who flaunted their contempt for decency so arrogantly. Having children of his own, he wished to keep his home free from Communist contamination. All his protests leading to nothing but insults and threats, he decided to take his family away to a little house in the country among some friendly peasants while making arrangements to get out of Russia. The more so, because the Soviet had appointed an official to look after his collection of paintings and ordered him to retire on account of " his bourgeois manner of describing the pictures of the post-impressionists to visitors ". By the time we quitted the house, the commissar had come to some arrangement with his two women, the ousted one making herself at home in my bedroom, thus obliging me to sleep on the divan in the adjoining study, while she claimed " communistic rights " over the commissar and by sheer force of vulgarity succeeded in establishing her foothold in the divided ménage.

Ivan Shookin, however, was loaded with demands for money by the local Soviet, " Make the bourgeois pay " being the slogan of the hour. Moreover, he was fined 50,000 roubles for " premature quitting of his apartment ", the report of which levy duly appeared in *Izviestia*.

Harassed almost out of his life, bullied from pillar to post, deprived of his money, the care of his precious paintings, which he had spent a life-

The Homes of the Mighty (Moscow)

time collecting, he found at last a means of getting abroad, happy at least in the prospect of living in poverty on the freedom-loving soil of France.

Some time after his departure, the Soviet broadcast to the world the lofty lie that they had opened for the first time to the public with various flattering arrangements the Moscow collection of post-impressionist paintings, while an eccentric Irishwoman, lulling her surging soul in the lap of Communist flattery, came back from Moscow with glowing descriptions of the gallery and what the Soviet was doing for art. Both the Soviet and its flatterer discreetly neglected to mention what had become of the wonderful old man who had devoted all his life, fortune and energy, to gather this collection, buying these " bourgeois " pictures from the painters when they were ignored and penniless. Nor did she dream of mentioning that while she was being feasted in those halls, the man who had adorned them was homeless and penniless in Paris, thrown out with insults and villainy by her smooth-tongued hosts.

Chapter XIV
A MIXED HOUSE

AFTER THE DEPARTURE of Ivan Shookin from his house I was obliged to seek shelter elsewhere. Fortunately a Russian friend came to the rescue and offered me a room in the flat he was occupying with his family in a large house near the Zoological Garden. I was fortunate in having so many excellent Russian friends, for during those long months of suffering, famine and persecution, I was never once given help by the British officials, who seemed to be quite indifferent to the fate of British subjects outside the circle of their own friends. It was the Russians, who themselves were losing everything, that begged me to share their last crust.

The room I now occupied was situated at the top of the house. The whole building originally belonged to a rich widow, who had been obliged to let off the top floor. We all shared a common dining-room, so that an opportunity was soon afforded me to watch the characters of the various inhabitants reveal themselves.

Marie Pavlovna, the rich widow, was a woman of

forty, of a radiant type that seemed to ooze rosy beauty. Short and plump, she had mouse-coloured hair and ash-coloured eyes that shone glassily. Diamonds shone ever in her ears and pearls looped her dove-like throat, while her silvery voice had always an echo of sootheless complaint. She was never without her male attendant. In fact, since her husband's death she had already installed a series of lovers. One had been a Belgian chauffeur, who finally went off with her motor-car and refused to return it. The present one was an ex-groom, who affected very sedate and immaculate clothes, large, white starched cuffs with diamond studs projecting conspicuously from his sleeves, as if to mark his change of station. The advantage of having this man for a "free" husband, as the term was, showed itself after the revolution, when the man promptly joined the Communists and was given the post of art commissar. In fact, the widow's house was full of art treasures which her late husband had collected. Nevertheless, this did not prevent Soviet searchers from entering the top flat, where my friend's aged aunt was arrested and taken to prison because she was found to possess a copy of the *Protocols of Zion*. She had had it ever since its first publication twenty years or so ago, and had merely got it out to read once again because every one was talking about it and marvelling at the astounding confirmation of all the protocol contained.

I do not know what became of the poor old

lady, for she was still in the Soviet prison when I left Russia.

We all had revolvers for defence purposes, and whenever there was a night search we were often obliged to hide them in the gutter of the roof just under the dormer windows. The penalty for possessing firearms was death, but so many marauding brigands were entering houses as commissars and murdering people that it was not safe to be without a revolver. On one occasion, a commissar opened my window to look for things that might be concealed on the roof, and it was only by knocking down a Sèvres vase and smashing it that I succeeded in drawing his attention back to the room for a few minutes, while I went to the window and brushed my revolver from the coping into the shrubs in the garden below. After that I devised a safer hiding-place for revolver and cash by removing the ikon which fills a corner crosswise in every Russian room and replacing it with a framed portrait of Lenin, placing it also crosswise like an ikon. On the little three-cornered shelf behind I hid the revolver and money. Whenever the Soviet searchers came into the room, they saw the picture of Lenin, murmured their approval and left me without further ado.

Marie Pavlovna's aged mother lived with her and was very fond of the old horse which used to draw her carriage in the old days. It had now grown old and decrepit and could hardly be kept alive because the peasants brought no corn or fodder to the town as a protest against the abolition of private trade and the nationalization of the products of the land. Everywhere one saw horses growing like bags of bones. Toorok, grandmother's horse, also became like a shadow, so rather than see him suffer any longer it was decided to kill him. A Tartar horseflesh dealer was called in, and from behind the upper window overlooking the stable-yard, the dear old woman stood watching the agony of her dear old horse. When the stream of blood flowed out from beneath the gate, she turned aside and wept.

There was also a little tragedy with one of Marie Pavlovna's Pekinese dogs. The stableman had a large wolf hound, but was unable to find sufficient food for its voracious appetite owing to the famine. He had been told never to let it out of the yard, but one evening it got loose and devoured one of the Pekinese almost at a gulp.

There was a small garden at the back of this house, where at evening the ex-groom "free" husband of the rich widow would bring various Soviet commissars. About that time there was a great stir in the population owing to the reported massacre of the Imperial family in July 1918. A requiem service which I attended at the church of St. Spiridon in the Spridonovsky Pereulok was the scene of extraordinary manifestations of popular sorrow. Fortunately for the priest, he happened to have been Vladimir Lenin's teacher of religion when the latter was a pupil at one of the colleges of Kazan. Everywhere one heard murmurs of indignation among the population. To counteract this, the Soviet leaders put forth a rumour.

At the Villa Charitonoff we heard it from the lips of a friendly commissar. He declared that it was true the Tsar had been shot, but that the Empress, the Tsarevich and the Grand Duchesses had been carried away to a monastery in a remote part, where they were being looked after.

This judicious rumour succeeded in allaying the great indignation of the people at the reported murder of the beautiful, innocent womenfolk.

A short while afterwards the *Izviestia* began to publish the diary which the Tsar had kept during his imprisonment. It was read with such pathetic interest by the population that it was discontinued.

Marie Pavlovna's aged mother was deeply religious and after the announcement of the murder of the Tsar, decided to beg the monks of the Donskoy Monastery to bring the ikon of the newly revealed " Samoderjhavnaya Virgin " (Autocratic Virgin) to her house for a *moleben* (short service). It was always the custom with pious Russians to invite a wonder-working ikon to their houses, where it would rest in the drawing-room on a white-covered table and the priests would incense it and chant litanies before it. It had become the vogue since the death of the Tsar to receive the " Autocratic Virgin " for this purpose. This ikon was miraculously discovered just after the announcement of the Tsar's murder. A woman had a vision in which the Archangel Michael revealed to her that an ikon of the Holy Virgin, crowned with the crown of the Autocrat of all the Russias, was walled up in a certain cellar. The woman related her vision to the monks of the Donskoy Monastery, a search was made, and lo, the ikon was discovered in the spot indicated in the vision. It was found adorned with the autocratic crown. This fact, coinciding with the death of the Tsar, brought the "Autocratic Virgin" into immediate popularity. Miracles began to multiply and the belief rapidly spread that this ikon had been especially revealed to signify God's approbation of autocracy. One sometimes wonders at the vagaries of Providence, but in this case it was obviously helping those who helped themselves.

The "Autocratic Virgin" was brought to our house by the priests and a very emotional service was held before it, the men and women weeping and sobbing when the old familiar prayers for the Royal Family were chanted. Even the ex-groom "free" husband and self-interested Communist was moved, for he turned to me and said in a shaken voice: "We have new masters, but all the same, the old had something so touching. It agitates the heart to remember. If 'God Save the Tsar' was to be played, I know we should all shed tears whatever we are, Communist or not."

Meanwhile from outside came the blare of the orchestra playing to an audience of the commissar aristocracy in the Zoological Garden, where concerts were given till far into the night, while the poor animals were neglected and starved to death. Later in the evening, after dusk, we heard the sound of shooting from the rear of the local Soviet. There were always these two sounds to remind us of the new régime, the shooting of political prisoners mingled with the blare of the orchestra at the neighbouring concert where the death-dealing commissars were being entertained after their day's work.

About this time a very unfortunate thing happened to the father of my friends. He had been living very quietly on the top floor with his wife and grown-up children. Being a landowner, his life was made a misery to him. The peasants had taken every scrap of land, and, urged on by a nasty pair of local Communists, who headed the Peasants' Soviet, insisted in making demands on the poor man's personal fortune for the various expenses of the estate. He was not even allowed to hide away from it in the town or to renounce the tax-obligations of the land and buildings he no longer possessed. This curious, perverse mentality was universal. Workers and peasants who had seized factories and farms still clung to the belief that the dispossessed capitalist was a sort of bottomless financial coffer, from which all demands connected with the confiscated businesses could be met. They gave themselves arbitrary wages, squandered the working capital, dismissed the management and set up their own, or in the case of land, broke up the large units and frittered them down by destructive division. Faced with disaster, they ran to the Government and the latter turned them to the dispossessed owners with the slogan: "Make the bourgeois pay!" The only way for the latter to escape from this madness was by fleeing abroad.

When M. Lvoff, my friends' father, fled from his estate, the Peasants' Soviet pursued him to his abode in Moscow. Then, finding their demands for cash were unavailing and that everything was being ruined on the estate, they sent a peasant to him with a very touching letter. In it they declared how sorry they were for having taken the land away, for all the wrong they had done, the insults they had offered, the cruel words they had spoken. They realized they had been led astray, that things on the estate could not be managed without the capitalist, that there were too many thieves and dishonest persons among themselves for anything to be run on communistic lines. They beat their brows against the ground, crossed themselves and swore by heaven that they were sorry and begged their old friend and master to return to manage the estate. They would elect him president of the Peasants' Soviet, and follow his advice in everything. "Beloved Pavl Nikolaich," they concluded. "With hot tears in our eyes, we look back to the good old times when you were always among us. You looked after our welfare and did everything so that nothing was neglected, nothing allowed to go to ruin, nothing done without order and foresight. Come back to us, beloved Pavl Nikolaich. We await you with bread and salt. We beg you."

Tears dimmed the eyes of M. Lvoff as he read

out the touching letter. His broad chest heaved and he embraced the bearded peasant Foma, who had brought the letter and stood with cap in hand in the little study.

"Noo da, barin," Foma declared, in a long, drawling voice, swaying his bobbed head. "Our heart is Russian. We have sinned, but the Lord is merciful to sinners. We repent with all our soul. Come back to us. You will live as before in the big house. We will come to you for advice as before."

M. Lvoff set off the same day for his estate in the Government of Tula. A few days later his wife received a letter from the same Peasants' Soviet, saying that they had locked M. Lvoff in the cellar of the house and would not release him until all the money had been paid which they had demanded. Madame Lvoff had no such amount in her possession, so, in despair, she dressed as a peasant, hiding her features with a kerchief, and went down to the village. Armed with a bottle of vodka, she went to the house under cover of dark, quickly made friends with the peasant-guard by taking the cork out and putting the vodka-bottle under his nose. When he was quite drunk, she smashed the lock of the cellar with a hatchet, rescued her husband and fled with him.

Her troubles, however, were not at an end, for, having an estate of her own in the Government of Vladimir, she was now pestered by demands for money by the miller's son and some of the village loafers, who had assumed all authority in the district as the " Soviet of the Poorest Peasants " in accordance with Lenin's decree. The estate had previously been run as a milk farm, while the forests supplied fire-logs for Moscow. The impudence of the loafer-expropriators knew no bounds. They were, however, no exception, for the same conduct was going on all over Russia at the express order of the Soviet Government. Besides making exorbitant and blackmailing demands for money, they carried on the milk business as their own and actually ordered Madame Lvoff not to get her supply of milk from any other quarter.

They acted in the same impudent manner regarding the fire-logs, which were a great business, requiring much foresight. Trees had to be felled, cut up, stacked and allowed to stand three years before they could be sent to Moscow for burning in the Dutch stoves. The Soviet scoundrels sold all the available stock and made no attempt to renew it. Moreover they had trouble with the other proletarians, the carters, for these considered the logs to be just as much their property as the Peasant's Soviet, and when they took them to Moscow they sold them on their own account. The same thing happened on most estates. The old bourgeois stock was sold and nothing done to replace it, so that Moscow and Petrograd were left without fuel and the people were obliged to tear down the wooden houses or chop up their furniture during the freezing months.

The Blue Steppes

Yet from their top windows they could see stretches of the vastest forests in Europe almost at the city's gates. How one could have laughed at "Communism", if it had not spelt so much misery and so many deaths to the unfortunate general population!

When the loafer-Soviet from her estate arrived to demand money, Madame Lvoff gave them a piece of her mind. The same evening she was arrested, kept in prison for three days and only set free after she had been condemned by the so-called "People's Tribunal" to a fine of 5,000 roubles "for counter-revolutionary abuse of members of the Soviet".

One day I was introduced to a Lettish anarchist, who was working with the Soviet. It was often my good fortune to be mistaken for an Irishman. The reason for this was that my passport, issued under the old régime, stated my religion to be Catholic. Russians have a curious way of deciding nationality by religion. Thus a Frenchman to them is always a Catholic, an Englishman always a Protestant, and an English-speaking Catholic must necessarily be an Irishman. I allowed them to foster this illusion, because the Bolshevists were giving every possible favour to the Sinn Feiners. Money was offered quite freely, for it was by encouraging the least loyal elements that the Soviet hoped to undermine the British Empire. I saw a list of names of Irish officers in the British army and navy who were marked down as "blagonadejhnie" (reliable), and I was asked to give the names of any others I cared to recommend as recipients of Soviet bounty! It was astounding. But later on, I saw the utility of this Soviet plan, for the failure of the Archangel expedition and the British Mission to Judenitch was largely due to the Soviet overtures to the Irish officers.

It was with this officer that I attended some lectures delivered in a large building known as the Officers' Economic Society in Moscow. The lecturer was the leader of the Anarchist Party, who had been working with the Communists since their rise to power. The Anarchists, however, began to discover that their conception of the State was very different from what was being put into practice by the Soviet rulers. After some eight months work with the Soviet, Lev Chorny, the Anarchist leader, suddenly expressed his views of the actual state of Communism at his lectures. He declared that Communism of the Marxian type was utterly foreign to the Russian character and that all true anarchists should stick to the interpretation of society delivered by Bakhunin. The Communist movement, he declared, had been entirely monopolized by the Jewish section, who were using it for the purpose of destroying national civilizations and affecting the supremacy of their own. According to him, the Jewish Sovietists looked upon the proletariats of the various nations as a " gelatinous mass ", entirely dependent for its shape and character on the nationally and historically conscious educated classes. By Communism, these latter would be removed in all countries and the masses would be left to the domination of the Jews, who would thus remove from the world the last vestiges of "persecution and sense of inferiority", to which they considered themselves subjected.

The argument concerning the value of the profession of faith of the intensely national Russian Jews in International Socialism had long agitated the minds of the Russian Socialists. The latter could not understand why the Jews should require a separate socialistic organization and suspected that they were aiming at economic advantages and tribal privileges, which were hardly compatible with the naïve conception of the Russian Socialists of a society in which no distinctions were to be made, no tribal coteries allowed. The question had been loudly discussed in 1905, when the Jewish Bund applied for affiliation to the Russian Socialist Party. The Russian Socialists naturally asked how there could be a strictly national party within a party that stood for the Russian proletariat as a whole. In the discussions which followed at the conference of the Jewish Bund, M. Litvinoff urged the Bund to enter the Russian Socialist Party, for then nothing would be lost but everything gained. Power, he declared, would pass into their hands. From inside they could arrange things as they wished, "the future being theirs".

According to Lev Chorny, the same thing had happened with the Communists. The Jewish section had secured power in the Communist Party and were using it for their tribal interests.

The curious part about this lecture is that it was the last the Anarchist leader delivered. He threw down the gauntlet without fear. During the night, however, the Soviet placed maxim-guns and cannon outside the headquarters and various buildings occupied by the Anarchists and blew them out without giving them a chance to hear or answer questions.

There was no doubt, however, that the Russian Jews took up Communism with a rare zeal as the solution of the Jewish problem. Not only did it offer them a chance to dominate the Gentiles, most of the commissars being Jews, while twenty-six out of thirty of the Soviet leaders were of the same race, but Communism was regarded by them as a wonderful means for advancing the Jewish race throughout the world and an infallible and downright means for removing from the face of the earth all the religious, economic, racial, social and other disadvantages under which the too sensitive Jews imagined they suffered. Communism was to clear the world of everything and everybody that wounded the intense national pride of the Jews. It was especially directed against Christianity, for the Russian Jew had an uncontrollable loathing of the mere name of Christ, and seemed never able to forget it. Many Russian Jews whom I met used to declare with frank cynicism that they did not look upon revolution as anything but " a change of ownership ".

The Blue Steppes

As for the Russian Jew as a type, he had played such an overwhelming part in the revolution and the Communist movement that no student of the Russian revolution can afford to close his eyes to the character of its ringleaders and propagandists.

I cannot do better than quote the words of a very shrewd Scotsman, who was in business in Russia for thirty-five years long before Bolshevism was heard of. In his book, *Thirty-Five Years in Russia*,[1] Mr. George Hume wrote in 1914: "The commonalty of the Jew in Russia has become the parasite of civilization, preying upon the vitals of the nation. It is an ingrained axiom of the lower class Jew that it is his religious duty to cheat the Christian, ... and, in very truth, for knavery, peculation, roguery, and disreputable dealing this type is unapproachable and unequalled."

This, then, was the type of Jew that flocked to "deepen the revolution" and prey in a gigantic, merciless way on the vitals of the Russian nation under the cloak of Communism.

All respectable Western Jews have, naturally, dissociated themselves from such people, just as respectable British citizens repudiate with scorn cut-throats and villains who happen to be of British nationality.

With my young Anarchist-Soviet Lettish aquaintance, I was able to see a good deal of the Soviet aristocracy, especially at its centres of amusement. Together we went one evening to a wooden

[1] Simpkin, Marshall & Co.

A Mixed House

villa among the woody suburbs beyond Petrovsky Park.

Driving up in a Soviet motor-car (confiscated from Princess Dolgorouki), we arrived before the villa which stood secluded among a group of tall pine-trees. The stars were shining overhead in the warm July night. Through the foliage of the surrounding trees could be seen the lights in the neighbouring villas, while the voices of strollers came from the sandy ways and paths. Yet the villa before us was all in darkness, the shutters tightly closed, the garden brown with pine-needles, dank and deserted.

Arvid, my Soviet companion, touched a bell knob and waited till a voice from behind the closed door asked for the watchword.

"Workers of the world unite," replied my Soviet companion.

The bolts were drawn and the door thrown open, letting out a flood of golden light into the blue night. The attendant was gorgeously attired in a livery after the style of the old régime. It was obvious a part of the dictating proletariat had to be set aside to wait on their "liberators". Footmen, immaculate in frock coats, took our hats with old-time obsequiousness. It was noticeable that they wore rosettes with the Soviet device, a sickle and hammer. What a farce it seemed to me, for not one of the Communist lordlings who came to the villa had ever touched a sickle or hammer!

The walls of the villa were plain logs, ornamented with foxes' heads and various skins of wild animals. The furniture was plain, mostly divans. In a large room we were introduced to various commissars with their women in various stages of matrimonial friendship. The show had not begun, for the greater part of the Communist revellers, all princes of the caste, had not yet arrived. We waited and chatted for about twenty minutes till there entered the most hideous collection of mortals that could ever come together. Russian Jews, Armenians, Caucasians, Tartars, Mongols, heaven knows what, all rulers of the Russian people, flocked in with their womenfolk, leaving their cars outside.

I was very much amused when a man went upstairs for a few moments and came back with a woman whom he introduced to the company with the explanation : " She is of Society ".

So it was evident the Communists had their own exclusive society from which the common proletariat was shut out. Perhaps this was quite natural, for it would be foolish to believe that the whole proletariat could enjoy the pick of the earth's riches. That was a privilege of a few, as in any form of society. In this Communist paradise, the Communists took the best of everything and did not forego their luxuries even though the rest of the country was starving. Truly, all that the Russian working-classes could say was that they had changed their masters and lost their liberty in the bargain.

The traditional gypsy band dispensed balalaika

A BOLSHEVIST FUNERAL.

"Glory to the fallen. Curses and Death to the hirelings of Capital.".

music, the usual toasts were drunk in champagne, glasses were smashed, the only difference being that a little red wine was mixed with the champagne in order to give it a revolutionary colour. Red roses adorned the supper table, red table cloths were spread and nothing but red sauces were served. Red speeches were made and one of the women, in her mad revolutionary enthusiasm (aided by the wine), declared that her one regret was that she could not grow a red skin. Nevertheless, she took consolation in being able to wear red next to her skin and produced a wave of ardour in the audience by jumping up on to her chair, lifting her red skirts and showing her red stockings.

With the increase of revolutionary enthusiasm and the consumption of the reddened champagne, tongues were loosened still more. Fiery speeches in most blasphemous language were made denouncing God, Christ, the Holy Virgin, Mahomet, Buddha, and all religions, against the kings and presidents of bourgeois countries, against morality and moral " prejudices ", while the world revolution, the Communist millennium and sex-communism were toasted and lauded, and death was called down on all the enemies of the Communist revolution. It was a terrible orgy of demoniac ideas and passions.

What the end of this revelry of the Communist ruling caste was I don't know, for I left soon after, anticipating the worst. A Soviet poet, Yessienin, the future twenty-five-year-old husband

The Blue Steppes

of Miss Isadore Duncan, recited some poems which were indecent to the last degree. I went out into the hall, took my hat and slipped out of the nefarious villa into the cool night air, alone. Never did the starry heavens and the blue night seem so lovely to me, so beautiful and holy after the vileness that was enthroned in the minds of those men and women in their mad desire to revolutionize the world.

Chapter XV

A BAG OF DIAMONDS

HOW I CAME to possess a bag of diamonds during the dark days of the Moscow famine and brought them safely to England, tucked away in the toe of my boot, still gleams in my shadowed memory like a glimpse of Ali-baba's cave. They were sparkling yellow diamonds, cut with a wealth of facets, clear and faultless as drops of dew, and all done up, the five of them, in a dainty blue silk bag shaped like a tiny heart, tied with a pair of tiny tassels, and adorned with the Imperial coat of arms and the name of Fabergé, the celebrated Court jeweller.

I ought to be a happy man. I have them still. I would not sell them for anything. But there's a tale behind them and I never take them out from their dark resting-place except on days of humiliation and regrets.

It happened in this way. There was a terrible famine in Moscow. Nobody except Bolshevist commissars and their people had sufficient to eat. The sovereign people were starving. The Soviet Government, having intentionally destroyed the value of the rouble by making it worthless, had decreed with egregious arrogance that the reign of gold and silver as a token of exchange was at an end, and that these "bourgeois" metals were henceforth to be used only for adornment and "dental purposes". This epoch-making blow at Capitalism was duly broadcast to the entire world by the Soviet wireless station and the event hailed in the egregious language of the Soviet as the crowning achievement of the socialist paradise.

This glorious fiction having been duly decreed from the Central Offices, reality stepped in to pay a little back in her own coin. The peasants sulked in their tents and refused to bring any food to the towns or to cultivate the soil for the mere delight of seeing the produce socialistically confiscated.

All of us, in those dark days, were obliged to forage for food, taking our old clothes and jewels down to the peasants and begging them to accept them in exchange for flour or potatoes. The Russian friends I was staying with at the time had no other means of keeping their big family of young sons and daughters alive except by sending the grown-ups into the country as "sackmen". They would go long distances with sacks on their backs, returning with potatoes or corn.

But there were other commodities that were equally necessary. There was sugar. One couldn't keep going without sugar in some form. There was none to be had anywhere, although one could stand and watch sackloads being taken into the houses of the Soviet officials under armed protection.

I was staying at that time with some people who had managed to keep the upper stories of their house near the Kremlin. The lower floor had been taken over for some sort of Soviet office of a military nature and the chief official, being an ex-officer and non-partisan, was favourably disposed towards the unfortunate "bourgeois" upstairs. In fact, his kindness was the means of saving part of Madame Peritonov's jewels. This lady was the aged grandmother of my young student friends. She had managed by various means to keep her last remaining jewels and valuables from the confiscating hands of the Bolshevists. But searches by day and night increased in frequency. Parties of soldiers, led by alien commissars, would arrive at all hours to search the house and remove all eatables and objects of value.

Madame Peritonov began to grow alarmed at the persistence and thoroughness of the searches. The commissars actually started to tear up the floor boards in search of prey. In order to put her little treasure beyond the reach of these vultures, Madame Peritonov begged the amiable ex-officer chief of the bureau on the ground floor to keep it in the office safe. He was delighted to do this and the friendship ripened so much that he used to come upstairs for tea every afternoon.

It was generally agreed that there must have been spies or traitors among the servants, for very soon after the jewels were stored in the official safe in the Soviet bureau, there was an attempt at burglary. The officer arrived next morning and found the place littered with papers, the cupboards broken open, and signs of hacking at the lock of the iron safe. So, after a little discussion, it was arranged that the heavy safe should be removed upstairs and deposited in the ante-chamber of Madame Peritonov's bedroom. She was too lame to go far from the room and would therefore always be on guard.

One night a group of soldiers arrived on a search. Their leader was a Polish Jew with restless ferret eyes. He saw the safe in the ante-chamber and, like a bird on its prey, he marked it for himself, abandoning all further search and ordering the men to carry it out into the night. He would listen to no protests that it was part of a Soviet office.

Though there was much grief in the house during the night, it departed the next day when the officer arrived and took immediate steps to recover the safe. Happily it was found unopened, although efforts had been made to force the lock. The Polish Jew, however, must have made a fortune elsewhere by means of confiscations, for the officer told us that he had left for Sweden, where he had been secretly transferring large quantities of precious stones. Had he been a Russian he would have been shot, but Jewish solidarity shielded him from all " persecution ".

After this episode, Madame Peritonov thought it

would be better to remove part of the treasure in case anything similar occurred again. Next time the confiscators might succeed in opening the safe, and she knew that for all their egregious talk of Socialism and the Proletariat, the Bolshevist commissars were very fond of adorning their womenfolk with the jewels and riches they took from other people. In this respect, too, the sovereign people were left to run behind the Soviet cars in rags and tatters, and with empty stomachs in the bargain.

Among the things Madame Peritonov decided to keep in her own secret hiding-place was the bag of yellow diamonds. When they were given to her from the safe, she laid them out on the tea-table, together with a rope of pearls, a heap of rings, and various other pieces of jewellery.

I took just a fleeting glimpse of them and never dreamt that the little blue silk bag with the yellow diamonds would one day be hidden in the toe-cap of my boot. It was sugar that caused it.

Madame Peritonov was anxious to get some for the sake of her small, growing grandchildren. There were so many of them, all between the ages of two and ten, and none of them had touched a bit of sugar for weeks.

Peter, a grandson of twenty-two, and Vassili, another of nineteen, had gone with me in search of sugar into all sorts of low haunts. There was none to be had. One day we had just come back empty-handed from a similar expedition, when the housekeeper came up from the kitchen with a look of triumph in her grey eyes. She had good news. Her nephew, a young married man and soldier in the Red Army, had just arrived. He was employed in the supplies section and could get sugar at a Moscow refinery whenever he cared to present his pass and orders.

Trunoff, for such was his name, was immediately asked to step upstairs. He came in, cap in his hand, dressed in an old army coat, blue-eyed, fair-haired and with a growth of yellow-stubble on his young face.

If the money was forthcoming, he could get as much sugar as they cared to have, though no quantity less than five pouds could be taken from the depôt.

A great confabulation was then arranged among the various heads of families. It was decided at last to pool resources and purchase five pouds. The price was 3,500 Tsarist roubles, equal at that time to about £200. Everyone was glad of the chance to get sugar.

Then, however, there arose the question of getting it home. Somebody would have to accompany the soldier both to take care of the money and to bring the sugar home. Trunoff suggested that an izvoschik would be sufficient as a conveyance.

But who would undertake the risk? It was a dangerous business. The Soviet had ordered all speculators to be shot. Madame Peritonov would not hear of either of her student grandsons undertaking the job. One could not hope to escape being shot unless one belonged to the chosen people.

At this remark everyone turned to me.

" Voilà votre homme ! " a bald-headed paterfamilias exclaimed. " He's English. They will not shoot an Englishman."

For some unknown reason I have never been able to explain to myself, I let myself be persuaded to go for the sugar. At that time I felt a great obligation towards Madame Peritonov for allowing me to sleep on the divan in her drawing-room and to share whatever could be found for the table. I was not allowed to leave the country, my belongings had been confiscated by the comrades while they kept me in prison, and my banking account had been "socialized". I had, however, a sum of money which I had been lucky to keep in my trunk in Petrograd, and with this I was able to provide for my wants, besides keeping a sum in readiness for the expenses of getting to England. For a small sum I was able to take my meals at Madame Peritonov's table and thus spare the money I would need later on. Perhaps it was a sense of repaying this kindness that caused me to undertake the risky job of bringing home the sugar. Speculation was rife. Bribery and underhand business were the only means of securing the necessities of life outside the circles of the Soviet. Since Socialism had taken everything for the State, which in practice meant the Soviet clique, everybody strove to take back what he could from the State, with as much scruple about ways and means as the latter had shown. Ownership having been declared communal, there was a terrible scramble for it. It was in this appalling atmosphere that I decided to carry the money and accompany the Red soldier to the refinery.

From the windows of the house, everyone watched us set out, raining signs of the cross upon our heads. Along the street Trunoff suddenly left me and spoke to a man wearing the uniform of a university student. They had a little chat and then Trunoff came back to me.

"That's my wife's brother," he said. "I wonder what he's doing hanging about here? He said he had just come from the station from a food expedition."

A little farther on he stopped at a street booth and bought some apples. He offered me one, but I refused it. Munching the apple and looking grim, he walked along towards the refinery on the banks of the River Moscow near the Kremlin. Before we got to the gates, he asked me not to come too near as there was a sentinel on guard who might look askance at a civilian. So I stood in the doorway of a house near by. The 3,500 Tsarist roubles were safe in my pocket. After a short while Trunoff came back and declared that the sugar was there, but that he would have to pay for it first. The office was just inside the gates. One could see the glass door if one stood in the middle of the road.

I gave him the money and watched him enter

the office door by the dozing sentinel. I watched and watched, waiting for him to come out again. . . .

A quarter of an hour went by and still no sign of him. I began to suspect that something was wrong. I ventured at last to ask the sentinel whether the soldier who had entered a short while before could be hunted up. The man called to a passing soldier and sent him into the office to inquire. He came back, saying that there was no sign of any soldier and that he must have gone out by the door on the other side of the building into another street.

Scenting treachery, I returned home to the man's aunt, who gave me his address, where his wife was sure to be found. I went there at all speed. At the door I asked the porter for Comrade Trunoff. He looked at me with slanting eyes.

"Comrade Trunoff?" he asked. "He left here, together with his wife, half an hour ago. They only hired one furnished room and took their belongings in a sack. A simple matter!"

I went back to the house with a dejected heart. So it was all a plot! What a land of misery it was! On all sides, in this socialistic paradise, was treachery, fraud, starvation, violence, hatred, murder, an avalanche of man's inhumanity to man, an endless welter of misery, while over all raved the Soviet fanatics with their fantastic fictions and paper promises, their bellowings of love for man and the ceaseless cracking of their guns against files of men.

Arrived at the house, I reported the full treachery

of Trunoff. There was a great outcry at the loss of so much money. It was not mine; I had merely consented to undertake the risky job so that none of the young members of the household should face the danger of being shot. But here, the relations of my student friends proved to be of a different mould from them.

"You must give us back the money from your own pocket," they said. "You should have had your wits about you."

They made a scene, a dreadful wailing, gesticulating scene. All my adventure in taking on that risky job was forgotten. Nothing but blame and reproaches were heaped upon my guilty head.

Well, what could I do? I hated scenes. I refused to discuss the matter. In the folds of my coat I had the Tsarist notes I had saved from confiscation and was keeping for my board and journey home. There were 6,000 roubles in all. I have been told by a Scotsman that I should have kept them in my pocket and gone away, but for some mysterious reason, a mere impulse, I took them out and handed 3,500 roubles to be redistributed among the discontented relations.

"Wait a bit!" said the bald-headed paterfamilias, who had first suggested me for the job. He counted the notes over with eager hands, wetting his fingers on his tongue. "There's a hundred missing."

I went out on to the balcony for a breath of fresh air. A feeling of suffocation was pressing at my throat.

A Bag of Diamonds

Madame Peritonov followed me out into the open. "I will pay you back half, if ever I get rich again," she said.

Her daughter, Madame Markoff, the mother of my student friends, Peter and Vassili, called out over her shoulder in an excited voice, waving her arms up and down:

"No! No! Every copeck! We will pay back every copeck!"

Towards evening, when the excitement had abated, Madame Markoff came to me with a subdued look and spoke in a quiet, pathetic voice.

"See here," she said, holding out the little blue silk bag. "It is a load on my conscience that you should have lost so much money. As you hope soon to go to England let me give you this little bag of diamonds. You will be able to sell them in London. We cannot do so here, as they would be confiscated by the Bolshevists. Take them with you. They will make up a little for what you have lost."

When the time came for me to make my exciting exit from the Russian slaughterhouse, I poked the little bag with the diamonds into the toe of my boot. It was a fearfully dilapidated old boot, for I had been obliged to mend it with my own hands with the felt of my hat. Such things were a common sight in the streets of Moscow, where the sovereign people walked about in mouldy, gaping footwear while their Communist rulers rode about in patent boots. But I didn't complain. I had a small fortune in my toe.

The Blue Steppes

I had a friend called Viola, a charming girl, who welcomed me back to London. When I told her the story of the sugar adventure, how dejected I had felt at Trunoff's treachery, how utterly miserable I had been at the ungratefulness of the bald paterfamilias and the rest, and finally, how happy when the little silk bag appeared as a token of nobler sentiments, she wished to see those diamonds. I had never shown or spoken of them to anyone. Their story was too full of reproach, too keen a reminder of human baseness and my own folly. But to her I told the story, for she was kind and angelic. And to her I showed the little blue silk bag with its Imperial coat-of-arms and its little nest of diamonds.

"Why do you keep them if they remind you of unpleasant things?" she asked as we sat at tea in Stewart's at the corner of Bond Street.

"Because they also remind me of the great relief I felt when they were offered to me and I realized that my friends were not ungrateful after all. In fact, Madame Markoff told me she wished to remove a load from her conscience, for it was in order to spare any danger to her sons' lives that I had consented to go for the sugar. It is not their value I care about, it was the *beau geste* with which they were given."

As we passed the windows of Spinks in Piccadilly my friend insisted on going in to find out how much they were worth. I yielded to this angelic pressure.

The man at the counter took the bag into a

A Bag of Diamonds

side window, took up a little instrument and fumbled with the diamonds. There was a pause and then his impulsive voice broke the stillness.

"They're glass!" he exclaimed.

And with that, one more glowing lamp was shattered in my life.

But, of course, she could not have known.

Chapter XVI
OUT OF THE JAWS OF HELL

I

WHEN I WAS SICK to death of the murdering, confiscating and odorous tyranny practised by the Soviet Government, I escaped across the frontier into Finland. I had attached myself to a party of Frenchwomen who were being evacuated from Russia. It was such a great joy to quit the blood-stained soil of the Soviet land that many refugees sank on to the sandy soil of Finland and thanked God for their deliverance. Not all, however, had time for such pious manifestations. They rushed along the railway track to the little station, and, bursting into the restaurant in scores, pounced like hungry wolves on whatever there was to be eaten. No preparations having been made for this sudden descent of refugees, there was little to be found. Three or four cold sausages lying under a glass cover were the object of a scramble among the hungry women which resulted in the smashing of the cover and the untimely division of the food. Never had I seen such unpleasant scenes. True, the dearth of food had been so great in Soviet Russia, the hunting for it so strenuous and competitive, that people were obliged to snap up whatever they could find. Not only in the matter of food, but with regard to all the commodities of life, the net result of Communism was to create an appalling scarcity of all things except Soviet arrogance and commissars, bombastic decrees and vain promises, while the acquisitive individualism of the citizens of this Communistic state was provoked to its highest and least agreeable point. The bait of profit and immediate gain, which the Bolshevists had held out to the people in their efforts to secure power, merely whetted the people's desire for possession after the Soviet was in power. The human side of these new citizens of the Communist State did not change one whit, and not all the drastic shootings ordered by the Soviet Government succeeded in instilling communistic, non-possessing principles into the baited people. Grab! had been the baiting slogan and grabbing remained ever after.

It is not surprising, therefore, that the spirit which had reigned so long in Soviet Russia should still manifest itself in these refugees.

Unfortunately for me, I was not even allowed to join the cry for food. Officials looked askance at me because I had no passport, and wished to detain me. I did not wait for argument, but in the general scrimmage boarded the waiting train and stayed there till it took me to the Swedish frontier. Here again I was held up. The Swedish authorities did not like passing a man without documents. I managed, nevertheless, to convince them that I was quite respectable, and they let me through.

Awaiting the refugees, both French and British, was a wonderful meal, offered by the British Minister at Stockholm. It was the first real dinner I had had for months, if I except those sumptuous repasts I was privileged to enjoy occasionally through being taken for a Sinn Fein Irishman and admitted to the exclusive society of the feasting Soviet officials.

Nothing was more obvious than the fact that any society, whatever it call itself, is made up of human beings with human appetites and desires, and that no society is run on decrees and negations alone. To starve the acquisitive instincts is merely to screw them up to the pitch of madness, and their repression in Russia, after they had been stirred up by propaganda promises, merely led to the ebbing away of the economic life of the country. When, to avert final collapse, the Soviet Government re-instituted a certain amount of private trade, there was such a rush amongst the population to do business that the Soviet was terribly alarmed at this upsetting of its communistic principle and immediately clapped hobbles on the mare. Which goes to prove that human nature remains the same for all the tyranny of Communism.

II

When I arrived in capitalistic England and saw the wonderful things that had been done in the

Out of the Jaws of Hell

way of social progress, I wondered how anybody could be so foolish as to dream of copying Russia. Here, under Capitalism, the position of the masses is so wonderful in comparison with Communist Russia and the removal of the evil legacies of the past so constantly effected by sure, if gradual, legislation that Communist Russia seems to me, who come from there, nothing but a conventicle of unscrupulous cant. I marvelled at the sight of the splendid houses erected under the various Government schemes in Britain and compared them with the ruin produced by Communism in Russia of the houses it had inherited from the old régime. Here hundreds, thousands of houses have been erected for the workers, while in Russia only a few have been constructed at the order of the Soviet Government for propaganda purposes and photographed. The pictures are distributed over the face of the world as " houses built by the Soviet for the workers ". A few houses copied millions of times in print! The only earthly paradise the workers can hope for is a Capitalist one.

The same trickery is practised by the Soviet Government in all departments. Factories, farms, houses, schools, children's colonies, homes, hospitals, etc., are all served in the same way. A few here and there are maintained at the expense of the State, photographed, written about, and shown to visitors who have secured a Soviet visa.

To step from such an atmosphere of cunning, deceit, falsehood, tyranny, bloodshed and endless violence into the practical, freedom-loving environment of Britain is like passing from the jaws of hell. Whatever her defects, Britain offers one the chance of progress, peace and the spirit of independence, instead of the hideous fangs of hatred and destruction, diabolical inhumanity and the crushing of every independent soul.

When I came back to England, I was surprised to find there could be anyone to approve of Communist Russia. I went into Hyde Park on May Day and stood beneath a platform where an orator was praising the glories of Soviet Russia. He declared that the accounts of Soviet atrocities were all manufactured in Fleet Street by the Capitalist Press. Having seen my friends brutally murdered, my belongings taken, seen the terrible sufferings of the vast majority of the Russian people and listened month after month to their whispered appeals, to hear this unscrupulous man was too much for me. I made a protest. Immediately a shoal of Russian Jews, wearing red ties, surrounded me, threatening and shaking their fists. I hated a scene and would have let the matter drop had not a British working-man tapped me on the back, saying: " Stick it, sonnie ! Tell 'em what you know ! "

There was a good deal of confusion and the man on the platform was interrupted.

" What's the matter down there, comrades ? " he asked.

" Here's a man says he's been in Russia," they answered.

Out of the Jaws of Hell

My working-men supporters demanded that I should be allowed on to the platform. The orator, however, disliked the idea.

" Look ! " he declared, in his most contemptuous voice. " A horny-handed son of toil ! "

The crowd laughed, and a Russian Jew put my Russian to the test. The crowd dropped into silence at this, and their wonder increased. Moreover, I produced some photographs of myself in Russia in the glorious company of commissars !

After that the orator placed his platform at my disposal on the insistence of half the assembly. As I went up the rickety stairs, he called out : " That's as near to heaven as you'll get." To which I promptly replied. " I quite believe it. The platform, you see, is yours."

Thereupon I held forth for about twenty minutes to a silent crowd chiefly concerning the ghastly fate of the workers who were imprisoned with me in Moscow because they had dared to strike and to maintain the traditional rights of trade-unionism.

As I walked away I could hear the orator, returned to his platform, addressing the crowd again : " Our comrade says . . . yes, I call him comrade. . . ."

I didn't stop to hear what he had to say further on my account. A number of working-men came to shake hands with me, thanking me for telling them how so many workers had been done to death by the Soviet Government for their independent stand and love of freedom.

From conversation with these men, I realized

that British working-men would never submit to be the slaves of the international tyrants that sit in Moscow.

But to me, steeped in the joys and sorrows of Russia, the memory of the blue steppes will always be like the grim shadow of a death-headed giant rising from the swamps and marshes of an Eastern land. . . .

www.ingramcontent.com/pod-product-compliance
Lightning Source LLC
Chambersburg PA
CBHW020224170426
43201CB00007B/313